swimming pools AND SPAS

By Curtis Rist, Vicki Webster, and the Editors of Sunset Books, Menlo Park, California

SUNSET BOOKS

VICE PRESIDENT, GENERAL MANAGER: Richard A. Smeby
VICE PRESIDENT, EDITORIAL DIRECTOR: Bob Doyle
PRODUCTION DIRECTOR: Lory Day
DIRECTOR OF OPERATIONS: Rosann Sutherland
RETAIL SALES DEVELOPMENT MANAGER: Linda Barker
EXECUTIVE EDITOR: Bridget Biscotti Bradley
ART DIRECTOR: Vasken Guiragossian
SPECIAL SALES: Brad Moses

STAFF FOR THIS BOOK

MANAGING EDITOR: Bonnie Monte
ART DIRECTOR: Vasken Guiragossian
SUNSET BOOKS SENIOR EDITOR: Sally W. Smith
WRITERS: Curtis Rist, Vicki Webster
COPY EDITOR: Carol Whiteley
PHOTO EDITOR: Dede Lee
PRINCIPAL ILLUSTRATOR: Tracy La Rue Hohn
PAGE PRODUCTION: Janie Farn
PRODUCTION COORDINATOR: Danielle Javier
INDEXER: Nanette Cardon/IRIS
PROOFREADER: Alicia Eckley
COVER PHOTOGRAPH: Dominique Vorillon

contents

the pleasures of a pool

Not so long ago, a backyard swimming pool was considered
the epitome of luxury—and with good reason. Pools were
expensive to install, and both time-consuming and costly to
maintain. As for spas, well, until the hot-tub craze swept
the country in the 1970s, few people outside California had
even heard of the things. In recent years, though, a couple
of trends have converged to change that picture.

a pool or spa for everyone

Over the last several decades, the concept of outdoor living has spread far beyond the Sunbelt. In addition, new products, innovative construction techniques, and hot competition in the industry have made swimming pools and spas much more affordable. The result: their popularity has skyrocketed, even in places where warm weather lasts for only a few months out of the year.

The photo gallery on these pages is designed to both fuel your imagination and show you some of the many practical options available to would-be pool and spa owners. Our "exhibit" includes pools that are literally works of art—personal statements whose creators spared no expense in their design, construction, and landscaping. (Those are the pools to dream of.) In other photos, you'll see examples that fall closer to home for most of us: pools and spas that are beautiful to look at and a joy to use while meeting the challenge of budget or space constraints.

▲ **BASICALLY BEAUTIFUL**

This no-frills pool, bordered by a colorful garden, sparkles like a jewel against the dark green of hedges and trees—proof positive that basic does not equal boring. A latticed moon gate adds elegance.

◄ **INTO THE WOODS**

Sensitive to their site, the owners of this property designed their pool to mimic a pond hidden deep in the woods. Shade-loving ground covers come right up to the rough stone coping.

◄ **HERE ON EARTH**
What could almost pass for a water-filled moon crater is (of course) a custom-designed spa with a broad coping and gently sloping deck of tinted concrete. Blooming tulips provide splashes of color while bearded-iris foliage echoes the strong vertical lines of tree trunks in the nearby pasture.

▲ MOUNTAINTOP MINIMALISM

Rectangles of plain concrete outline this pool-spa combo and form the nearby patio. The owners took such an ultra-low-key approach for a very good reason: to give center stage to the stunning mountain views and dramatic outdoor sculpture.

▶ SPRING FLING

Even a plain wooden hot tub takes on a festive air when it's surrounded by well-tended trees and pots of golden daffodils. When the spring bulbs have passed their prime, they'll make way for colorful annuals.

◀ MEDITERRANEAN IDYLL

With its raised coping of rose-tinted concrete and wall of vibrant tile, this pool is a beautiful complement to the Spanish style architecture of the house. The Mediterranean theme continues in the dense screen of container plants at poolside.

▼ A PERFECT MATCH

The most visually pleasing pool designs work hand in glove with the homes they adjoin. Here, the sharp angles, light colors, and broad planes of the house are echoed in those of the pool and decking. The result: a textbook example of getting it right.

▶ RUGGED CHARMER

The jagged contours and earthy shades of stone hold sway in this rustic setting, from the pool house walls to the rough-hewn decking. Even the ladder rails have been carved from stone.

▶ A UNIFIED LOOK

This spa (right) is ideally suited to its formal landscape thanks to a facing of mellow brick that matches the retaining wall.

▶ ON THE BEACH

Maybe you can't have your own secret lagoon, but you can have the next-best thing (far right): a swimming pool that looks like one, complete with "sand" made of textured and tinted concrete.

▲ YEAR-ROUND FUN

At one time, an indoor swimming pool was something most of us could only dream about. Now, especially in cold-winter regions, these four-season playgrounds are common sights—thanks in large part to new, more affordable materials such as those used to build this pool's shelter.

◄ TWO OF A KIND

A shared coping of flagstone gives a custom look to this standard pool and spa, tucked into a thickly wooded hillside. Masses of deep-rooted, shade-loving plants both soften the edges and, more important, help stem erosion on the steep slope.

▶ **SOMETHING SPECIAL**

Vinyl pools come only in standard shapes, but that doesn't mean you can't create a one-of-a-kind look. Here, that feat was accomplished by nestling a standard spa into the pool's bend, laying down an elegant stone deck, and adding pool-side structures in the same mellow gray tones.

▼ **ABOVE AND BEYOND**

A simple extension of the house's deck transforms this above-ground pool into an integral part of the landscape.

▼ **BOTTOMS UP**
An almost-vertical hillside ensures privacy
and security for the owners of this pool.
Dense plantings and a sturdy retaining wall
keep the soil firmly in place.

▲ **DESERT LIGHT**
Dozens of lights set just below the level
of the coping are barely noticeable
by day; at night, they turn the desert
landscape into a magical backdrop
for pool and patio.

◄ **LESS IS MORE**

In close confines like those of this courtyard, success lies in the details—in this case, a trio of mythical beasts, a few plants of mammoth proportions, and a simple palette of deep green and deep blue against pale stucco walls.

17

◀ CLASSIC SIMPLICITY

With ever-changing patterns cast by classical sculptures and surrounding trees, this simple rectangular pool is used more for meditative viewing than for swimming.

▼ STEPPING DOWN

The owners of this house found an innovative solution to a dauntingly steep site: a multilevel spa set into a deck high above the ground.

NOW YOU SEE IT
The terrace around this beach-front pool features a sliding wall. Closed, it ensures security and privacy; open, it lets swimmers enjoy the view of sand and sea.

▲ WATER ON EDGE

An infinity-edge pool makes a stunning landscape feature on a terraced hillside. Seen from the deck, the far rim of the pool simply vanishes. On the side facing the lawn, a sheet of water falls over the wall into a catch basin, where it is recycled into the pool.

▶ KEEP IT SIMPLE

Even if budget is not a factor, a basic above-ground pool is the perfect option for renters or those who want a pool they can easily remove when their children are grown.

▶ **LAKE IN THE WOODS**
A lavish use of native stone and dense plantings that come right up to the water's edge provide exactly what the owners of this pool wanted: a dead ringer for a bend in a river.

▶ **VIEW WITH A POOL**
Glass-panel railings serve as secure, solid balusters without blocking views of the pool and garden. Sheets of tempered glass are set in a deep channel cut into the decking.

▲ EASY DOES IT

In a courtyard designed for relaxing, the sight and sound of water take center stage. The pool's gently curving side echoes the lines of the terra-cotta planters and clay roof tiles.

▶ **SITTING PRETTY**

A red sofa adds a vibrant spark to a palette of dark green and pale blue while offering pleasure in triplicate: cozy seating, shade overhead, and a water view.

▼ **DESIGNED FOR DUNKING**

At a home on the edge of Puget Sound, a duo of dipping pools— one hot, one cold—was designed for pleasure and practicality. Swimmers fresh from the beach wash off in the cold pool before they sink into the hot one.

▶ A FRAGRANT SOAK

In a spa surrounded by sweet-smelling flowers, soakers can bask in the joy of both warm, relaxing water and beautiful scents.

A color scheme of brown, white, and palest gray sets a tone reminiscent of summers long ago. The shades repeat in the big shingled house, inviting wicker chairs, picket fence, and the simple stone coping around the pool.

▲ **LOG CABIN LAP POOL**

Snug inside their log house, the owners of this lap pool and spa can enjoy the water right through the coldest winter days. Sun streaming through the glass and skylight keeps the stone deck warm enough for barefoot comfort.

▶ **SOOTHING SAUNA**

Spending even a few minutes in a sauna can relax tense muscles and ease everyday stress. While your body and psyche enjoy the health-giving benefits of the heat, the softwood walls and benches remain comfortable against your skin.

▲ MAGIC CARPET

With infinity edges on two sides, this pool seems to float above the valley far below. The walls beneath those vanishing rims function much like building facades: although they can't be seen from the house, they often figure as prominent features in the land-scape and demand as much thought as the rest of the pool's design.

◄ LEAN AND SLEEK

Clean-lined and simple, this lap pool is perfectly suited to the stark, modern lines of the pool house. The vine cloaking one side of the wall has started across the slatted overhang; eventually it will provide welcome shade.

BLUE ON BLUE
Like many vanishing-edge pools, this one has been positioned to blend with the watery vista beyond. It has also been tinted to match the deep blue color of the lake on a sunny day.

planning a pool or spa

A backyard swimming pool used to mean one of two things: an in-ground rectangle or an above-ground circle. Today, thanks to new technology, there are countless design options to choose from. Spas, too, offer a wealth of choices, from those that can be set up in minutes to in-ground units that connect to swimming pools. But before deciding on the style, shape, and materials for your pool or spa—which we'll get to in the next chapter—you'll need to think about these factors first: how you intend to use your pool or spa, what the costs will be, where you will place it, and which contractor you will use. Let's take an in-depth look at each of these areas.

how you'll use your pool

The first consideration in planning a new pool or refurbishing an existing one is how you plan to use it. Maybe you want an area for guests and entertaining, or simply a fun spot for recreation with the kids. Perhaps you're interested in some serious exercise or even physical therapy. While pools can serve multiple functions, focusing on your principal needs and wants will help you choose wisely as you work on placement and positioning in your yard or home.

RECREATION

Recreation is the key reason most people build a pool. After all, who doesn't want to cool down in hot weather and have a wonderful place to while away the hours? If your goal is spending weekends with your family in a pool filled with inflatable toys and perhaps a floating lounge chair, that might suggest you don't have to construct the most luxurious model. A lower-cost version, such as an above-ground pool, may suit you—and still leave plenty in the budget for swimming lessons.

Nor is a deep pool essential—especially if young children are involved. For example, if you want to play water volleyball and swim the occasional lap, a constant depth of 4 feet should be more than adequate—deep enough to splash and swim in, yet shallow enough to provide safety for all ages.

EXERCISE

While splashing about in even the shallowest of pools provides some exercise, serious athletes and those looking for the therapeutic benefits of water exercise will probably want a lap pool. Olympic pools are 50 meters (about 164 feet) long, but it's not necessary to build

A well-planned pool satisfies many needs at once. Combining good looks with manageable size, this simple pool set into the corner of a yard maximizes the possibilities for safe recreation.

A pool intended purely for exercise doesn't require extensive room around it for socializing. This lap pool makes excellent use of a long, narrow space among mature trees.

If your goal is simply to have a handy place for family fun, there's no need for a high-end installation. A modest above-ground pool like this one is a crowd pleaser.

anything that size. A pool ranging from 25 to 40 feet will allow a swimmer to execute several swift butterfly or freestyle strokes before having to reverse direction. For lap swimming, a depth of 3½ feet is adequate.

For water aerobics and other forms of exercise, such as jogging with a float belt, you'll need a pool that's deep enough to tread water without constantly touching the sides or the bottom—in most cases 5 or 6 feet should suffice. Likewise, if the pool is to be used for physical therapy, you may not need an overly deep one.

One excellent option for accommodating the need for exercise is a swim spa. This is

to dive or not to dive

■ ■ ■

Including a diving board or slide is a tempting option, but both raise a long list of concerns—and many pool contractors refuse to add them. To avoid injury, a pool with even a low diving board needs an area at least 9 or 10 feet deep that extends out at least 12 feet in front of the diving board. In all cases, pools with diving boards must be built according to the safe-diving specifications developed by the National Spa and Pool Institute (see "Resources" on page 218). Diving boards and slides may require additional liability insurance, and will certainly require more intensive supervision of children using the pool.

literally a small pool—as small as a dozen feet long—in which, with the flick of a button, a pump creates a powerful water current that the swimmer moves against,

swimming in place. Although swim spas can be built outdoors, they can also be brought indoors thanks to their compact size (see more about swim spas on page 75).

ENTERTAINING

If hosting outdoor gatherings is factored into the mix, you'll have a few additional considerations. Not only will your pool need to function well and be an inviting and safe place for recreation, you will want it to look exceptionally good, too. While this may not alter its overall function and form, it will certainly affect your decisions about how to approach landscaping.

For example, you may not only choose to surround the pool with a deck or patio but also to connect it to the house for access to the kitchen and indoor bathrooms. You may also want to add structures to hide pool equipment as well as a pool house to provide changing areas. Clearly, a pool used for entertaining can grow into a much larger project.

RELAXATION AND THERAPY

Floating in a pool or sitting in a lounge chair alongside one can certainly be relaxing. An even better way to unwind is to step into a spa or hot tub. These units take two major forms: either in-ground or portable (also known as above-ground).

An in-ground spa is almost always connected directly to a swimming pool and shares the pool's water filtration and heating equipment. For a spa that won't be linked to a pool, the portable variety makes the most sense. It requires no excavation and can be located nearly anywhere, even indoors. Often, people build

In many cases, a swimming pool serves as a backdrop for outdoor entertaining, as in this idyllic setting where guests are just as likely to congregate on the covered terrace as in the pool itself.

The churning waters of a heated spa can indeed be relaxing. These two in-ground spas sit close to the house, making them inviting for a spur-of-the-moment soak. Attractive landscaping heightens the pleasurable effect. A wisteria-covered arbor (above) provides a fragrant canopy for bathers. The small seating area near the naturalistic spa (right) encourages gathering after a dip.

decking around a portable spa to give it the look of an in-ground spa without requiring any digging.

Because portable spas have the necessary pipes, filters, and heaters built in, setting them up is usually quick. In fact, some portable tubs truly rank as do-it-yourself projects that anyone can tackle—you simply plug them in, fill them with water, and begin soaking.

the effects of hot water

■ ■ ■

Water—especially hot water from a spa—helps relax the body by warming muscles and causing blood vessels to dilate; the effect can be similar to having a massage. Still, spas aren't for everyone. Those with heart disease or blood-pressure disorders or women who are pregnant should consult a physician before stepping into a spa.

calculating the costs

While swimming pools do rank as luxuries, the costs—and the possibilities—have changed so much in recent years that there is a pool for almost every budget and need. Just remember to include auxiliary expenses such as maintenance and additional insurance when determining the total cost of the pool.

OPERATING COSTS

Operating a pool or a spa can lead to some surprising expenses, beginning with the water to fill it. Given that the average pool holds approximately 20,000 gallons of water, the cost can be considerable. If you install a water heater, you need to include fuel costs, along with the cost of electricity to operate the filtration and purification systems. Fuel and electric rates vary widely in different parts of the country, but, depending on your location and climate, operational costs for a pool or spa can add hundreds of dollars to your monthly utility bill.

Even if you live in a warm area of the country, it doesn't automatically mean you'll have a lower overall energy bill. In Florida, for instance, it may cost more to heat a pool than it would in Illinois, because you'll be using the pool year-round rather than just four or five months a year. The best way to avoid sticker shock is to check with pool owners and pool builders in your area. Ask to see actual bills that can help you estimate what your costs might be.

This simple, tasteful pool (right) eschews frills in favor of practicality. It creates a comfortable, spacious zone for recreation using far less costly materials than the pool shown above.

installation costs

While the specific costs for constructing a pool or spa vary by region as well as by season, here are some broad price guidelines. These numbers reflect minimum costs; special materials, equipment, or landscaping will raise the prices.

TYPE OF POOL	COST
Basic above-ground pool	$6,000–$8,000
Large above-ground pool with deck	$10,000–$12,000
Basic in-ground pool lined with vinyl	$18,000–$20,000
Basic in-ground pool made with gunite	$22,000–$27,000
Basic in-ground spa pool made of fiberglass	$25,000–$30,000
Rectangular lap pool	$25,000–$30,000
Gunite pool/spa combination	$30,000–$35,000
Gunite pool/spa combination with waterfall	$40,000–$45,000
Portable spa	$2,000–$4,000
Wooden hot tub	$4,000–$6,000
In-ground spa	$8,000–$10,000

The possibilities for creating a pool with a high sense of style are virtually limitless. In this lavish pool, the stunning mortared wall and architectural elements create the aura of a palatial room.

cost-saving tip

When creating a budget, one way to manage the costs is to proceed on the project in phases. Build the pool or spa first, putting basic electrical and plumbing necessities in place. Later you can upgrade by adding heaters, automatic cleaners, and lighting, as well as decks, patios, landscaping, and a pool house.

MAINTENANCE COSTS

The pristine waters of a beautifully maintained swimming pool can be a delight to look at and jump into. Keeping that water fresh looking, however, takes work and a financial commitment. Without maintenance, a pool or spa will quickly become an algae-filled pond. You'll need to keep the water chemically balanced and sanitary, maintain the filtration and heating equipment, and clean the pool edges and surrounding patio or deck surfaces. As many homeowners discover, the amount of time this requires can often equal—if not exceed—the amount of time they actually spend swimming in the pool.

The many advances in pool-maintenance equipment, which are discussed on pages 176–199, can make the pool easier to take care of. But the initial cost of such equipment can easily double the price of the pool itself. Another option is to hire a pool service company to do the work for you. Either way, thinking about these expenses in advance can help you determine which size pool or spa best suits your budget as well as your needs.

Beyond basic rectangles and ovals, pools can be created in any shape imaginable. The strong geometry of this pool (right) is an example of how striking originality can emerge from a bold plan and the simplest of materials.

increased property value

■ ■ ■

For many years, swimming pools were considered a liability when it came to selling a house. Today, however, a well-constructed and landscaped pool is the opposite. Because of easier clean-up and automated maintenance systems, as well as more tasteful construction that ties a pool to the landscape, pools are often seen as an asset.

While there may be no difference between an in-ground pool and an above-ground pool regarding enjoyment value, there is usually a very real difference when it comes to property value. A well-designed in-ground pool is a permanent structure, adding greatly to the assessed value of your home as well as to its appeal for most future buyers. As a result, you can expect your taxes to rise proportionately following a visit from the tax assessor. An above-ground pool can sometimes be exempted from these taxes, since it is considered a temporary structure. But it is also not likely to add much value to your home, and may even detract from its value if you should sell. Before you build, it's a good idea to check with neighbors who have a pool to learn their experiences in your community.

LIABILITY COSTS

As much fun as they can be, pools and outdoor spas pose an additional liability risk. Most communities have zoning laws that govern safety—such as requiring fencing around the pool or having a cover in place when the pool is not in use. While these are worthwhile regulations, they entail some expense. Even something as innocuous sounding as a fence can cost thousands of dollars to install. Your homeowners' insurance premiums are also likely to rise if you add a pool, especially the liability portions. Such costs vary widely, and the only way to accurately gauge the increase is to ask your insurance agent.

choosing a pool location

In the past, pool shapes were limited, which restricted the possibilities for positioning one on your lot. Nowadays, though, the variety of stock models available, as well as the ability to create a free-form pool for the same price as a rectangular one, means that there is a pool for nearly every lot.

THINKING ABOUT LOGISTICS

Pay attention to privacy when you think about where to locate your pool. Placing the pool along the street or right next to the neighbor's yard may not make the most sense—although any area can be screened by making clever use of plantings and fencing. Also consider the position of the pool with respect to your house. Even if you intend to build a pool house for changing, easy access to your home is a plus. A pool located far from the house, or near an inconvenient entrance, such as the front door, can complicate matters.

Another point to consider is access for large construction equipment. While this is not a factor in planning an above-ground pool or portable spa, it becomes essential in helping to determine the location of an in-ground pool. The equipment can't pass over certain obstructions, such as septic tanks, and in general demands a 10-foot-wide access route equivalent to a driveway. In cases where the rear of a lot is inaccessible, it may even require careful negotiations to obtain a construction right-of-way through a neighbor's yard.

important!

For obvious safety reasons, swimming pools and spas can't be located beneath overhead power lines. If need be, the power lines can be moved or buried underground—though doing either will add to the cost of the project.

The placement of a pool greatly affects its ambiance. Built close to the house, this pool becomes a very public meeting place.

PLACING A POOL ON A STANDARD LOT

Just because a lot is a conventional shape, such as a rectangle, it doesn't mean that the pool you build has to be, too—although it certainly can be.

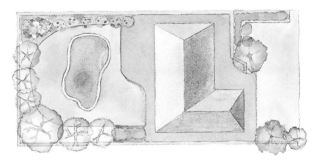

NATURALISTIC POOL
Ringed by a glade of trees, a naturalistic pool creates a forest setting in a small garden.

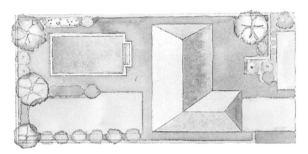

RECTANGULAR POOL
A rectangular pool and a spacious sheltered lawn form two separate backyard recreation areas.

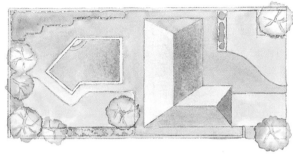

ANGULAR POOL
With the adjacent lawn echoing its contours, this angular pool produces a strikingly contemporary environment in a conventional backyard.

PLACING A POOL ON AN ODDLY SHAPED LOT

Since an in-ground pool can be constructed in any shape, an oddly shaped lot can actually lead to the creation of a unique and beautiful pool.

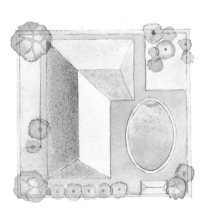

SQUARE LOT
An elliptical pool softens this lot's severe geometry and serves as an elegant focal point in the backyard.

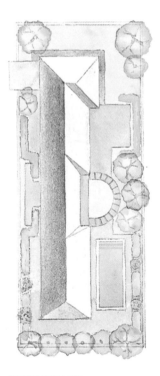

SHALLOW LOT
Creating a number of focal points across the width deepens an extremely shallow lot. This one has a central rounded patio ringed with trees, a rectangular pool and spa on one side, and an entertainment terrace on the other.

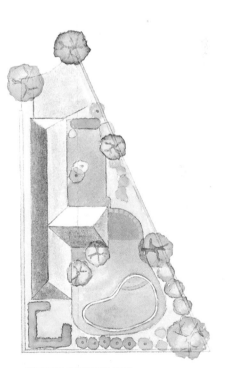

WEDGE-SHAPED LOT
Irregular outdoor spaces lend themselves to distinct activity zones. The generous pool area in one corner provides space for a multitude of pool-related activities. A smaller patio area near the front is private and intimate.

choosing a spa location

Compared with swimming pools, which must be carefully sited based on many factors, spas generally offer far more versatility in terms of where they can be located. Although an integral spa has to be adjacent to a swimming pool, portable spas can be positioned anywhere, even indoors. This can be a boon in colder climates if your goal is to use the spa year-round.

INSTALLING A SPA OUTDOORS

Although a spa can be located just about anywhere outdoors, it makes sense to install it next to a swimming pool. It's often desirable to provide more privacy for the spa, however, in the form of fencing or screening, and it may also be necessary to shelter the spa to protect it from winter chill.

In addition, a spa needs a flat surface that can support not only its own weight but the weight of the water it is filled with—which can add thousands of pounds. Placing it on a deck may be an option, but the deck has to be properly constructed in order to handle the load. You may need to call in a contractor or structural engineer to make the determination. Portable spas can't be placed directly on the ground, since their sheer weight will cause them to settle unevenly over time. Instead, many manufacturers require their spas to be installed on a 4-inch concrete platform, which can be placed or poured on the ground. Keep in mind that the term "portable spa" actually refers to the ease of delivery and installation. Once these spas are installed, they cannot be moved easily.

Outdoor spas can range from the fanciful, such as the one at left that's set into a garden paradise, to the functional, such as the spa above built on the edge of a stone terrace.

INSTALLING A SPA INDOORS

Because of the need for privacy and the desire to use the spa year-round, many people opt to have their spa indoors. Here, there are several concerns to address, the first of which is the size and weight of the water-filled unit. To be certain the floor is strong enough to support the thousands of pounds of additional weight, you may need to consult a contractor or structural engineer. In addition, the size of the spa has to be considered, because of the difficulty

A thoughtful setting augments the soothing nature of an indoor spa. Some possibilities include siting it in a plant-filled conservatory (above), or making it the focal point of a separate room, as in this traditional Japanese-styled home (right).

in maneuvering the unit up stairs and through doorways. Although it may be portable, it is hardly small. Finally, think about the best location in the house. Spas, like bathtubs, can create a watery mess around them. Make sure yours is in a room that can be cleaned easily and that can withstand trails of water.

a look at the weather

Besides picking a location that's accessible for construction and convenient to use, two other factors demand consideration: the sun and the wind. Regardless of your climate, giving some thought to these elements can result in a pool or spa that is more comfortable in warm weather and can help extend the swimming season in colder climates.

Where temperatures are high, the shade of tall trees provides welcome relief during the heat of the afternoon.

FACTORING IN THE SUN

In most situations, the ideal swimming pool or spa location has a southwest exposure that allows the maximum amount of sunlight at all hours. Although the pool will likely be shadowed in the morning, this probably won't bother early-rising swimmers, who are usually hardy souls. But be sure to take into account your particular climate, since a southwest exposure may not be optimal for your circumstances.

In desert areas where overheating is an issue, a pool facing east or even north will provide some relief from the intense sun. (In addition, plantings that shade all or a portion of the pool can help to make things bearable.) In northern areas that are comparatively cool in the summertime, a full southern exposure can provide you with more hours of enjoyment in the pool and reduce the cost of heating the water.

tracking the sun

■ ■ ■

An understanding of the daily and seasonal patterns of sunlight and shade created on your property will help you place your pool to make maximum use of the available sunlight during swimming hours. Observe and record the sun's movement and effects. And remember that the high summer sun tends to create short shadows and that the lower sun of spring, winter, and fall casts longer shadows—which can impact the pool.

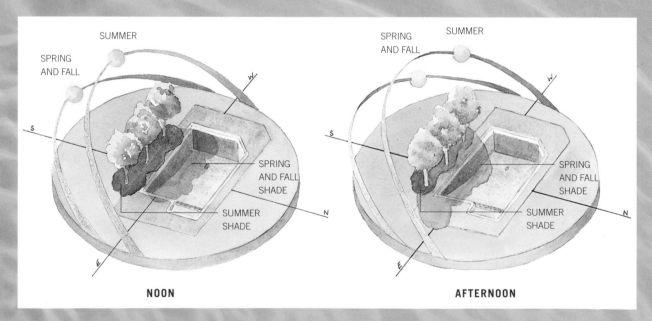

SUMMER

SPRING AND FALL

SPRING AND FALL SHADE

SUMMER SHADE

NOON

SPRING AND FALL

SUMMER

SPRING AND FALL SHADE

SUMMER SHADE

AFTERNOON

TAMING THE WIND

Wind can greatly affect the perceived warmth of a pool or spa as it ripples across the water—and is nearly as important a consideration as sunshine. Too much wind blowing across the area can be unpleasantly chilly, and too little can create a stagnant space on a sweltering day. The ideal is to strike a balance: having a gentle breeze without steady winds or a stifling atmosphere.

Winds vary from region to region, and even from property to property. Some areas of the country are subject to prevailing winds that blow constantly for weeks. Other areas experience daily breezes at particular times of the day. One way to determine the situation in your area is to set

A solid fence isn't the only way to block harsh winds. This transparent screen shelters the pool from the elements without blocking the beautiful view.

up small flags and watch how they move over time, recording your observations. This will help you place the pool or spa for maximum advantage. Fences can also divert and soften the force of breezes (see page 149).

43

the lay of the land

Two more factors that require careful attention in the construction of a pool or spa are soil and slope. While neither one will likely be extreme enough to eliminate the possibility of building a pool, both can influence your design choices as well as the overall cost of the project.

UNDERSTANDING SOIL TYPE

Once you've chosen the site for your pool, you may need to have a core sample of the land drilled and analyzed by an expert. An experienced pool contractor will be familiar with this process, and can either make the analysis or enlist the help of a soils engineer.

GARDEN LOAM The is the ideal soil. It's easy to dig and drains well.

SANDY SOIL This type of soil is composed of large particles and is easy to excavate. But the walls of the hole tend to collapse during the process. Excavators may need to prop up the sides of the hole with wooden supports or else spray the walls with concrete to hold them in place as the job proceeds.

CLAY SOIL This too can be problematic. Consisting of very small, tightly packed particles, clay soil expands when wet, putting tremendous pressure on the finished shell of the pool. This may require extra strengthening with steel or counteracting the force with additional concrete.

BEDROCK Contractors may need to resort to dynamite to blast the hole for the pool, which can greatly increase construction costs.

A MATTER OF DRAINAGE

Whatever the texture of the soil, if it remains wet because of groundwater, excavation will be difficult; as soon as the hole is dug, it will fill up with water. A remedy for this is a drainage system, and possibly even a sump pump that will remove water as excavation continues; however, both can add hugely to costs. Depending on the severity of the wetness, the drainage system may have to be left in place permanently to prevent groundwater from undermining the pool.

In addition, the area around the pool should be sloped so that rainwater runs away from the pool or spa. Sometimes, drainage pipes are laid beneath the pool decking on top of a gravel bed; gravity then draws the water away from the area (see illustration below). Depending on where the pipe leads, it may be necessary to add a sump pump to remove the accumulating water. Building either system correctly—whether for draining groundwater or for draining rainwater—requires a skilled contractor.

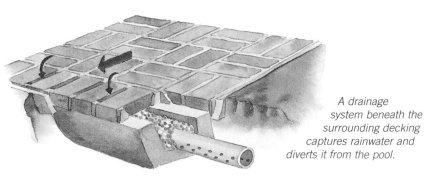

A drainage system beneath the surrounding decking captures rainwater and diverts it from the pool.

WORKING WITH A SLOPE

Few yards are perfectly level, and, in fact, some of the most spectacular pool settings are those built into steep hillsides or even cliffs, with the pool held in place by concrete and steel piers or suspended and cantilevered from below. When designed well, such pools can be magnificent.

Building a pool into a hillside requires special preparation, since the pool needs to be engineered and constructed to withstand the pressure of the earth piled on one side and to support the free-standing section on the other side. On the downward-slope side, the pool needs to have a solid foundation, similar to the concrete footings that strengthen and support the typical house foundation. In areas where there is bedrock beneath the soil surface, the pool structure can literally be connected to it with giant steel pins. However, retaining walls may be needed on the upward slope to prevent erosion, which would weaken the structure. Such walls may also be needed to resist tremors in areas that are prone to earthquakes. In all cases, a retaining wall higher than 3 feet should be engineered by a professional, and may require special permits.

Despite the difficulties posed by construction, a steep slope sometimes proves to be an asset, creating a spectacular setting for a pool or spa. Here, the resulting pools form a seamless connection with the ocean (upper right), the mountains (right), and the wilderness (below).

money-saving tip

Even if your particular soil or slope conditions aren't ideal, a swimming pool can almost surely be built on your site. Before proceeding, however, you should ask the contractor how much extra it will cost to build a pool under the particular conditions. In some cases, the additional work needed to compensate for the slope or the soil type can exceed the actual cost of the pool itself.

plans and permits

Professional designers and pool contractors can select a site for your pool based on a survey of your yard. However, the more information you have and the more opinions you can present to them, the smoother the process will be.

DRAWING A PRELIMINARY PLOT PLAN

On your own, begin by making a plot plan of your property, an overhead view drawn to scale. You can use low-cost computer software to make elaborate 3-D representations, or you can make a simple scale drawing of your property on graph paper with the location of your house sketched in.

If your house and land have already been surveyed, as most have, you can use the survey map for this process; often it's attached to your deed.

Mark the location of your house, along with other features to consider, such as driveways, garages, and any outbuildings, as well as septic fields and septic tanks. Think of the sun exposure, the wind, soil conditions, and any slopes, and mark these on the map in terms of whether they are favorable or unfavorable.

Then you can use tracing paper to experiment with different swimming pool shapes and locations (see below). This approach allows you to work through various sketches without having to redraw the base plan as you change your ideas. When you meet with a designer or pool contractor, arrive with pictures from books and magazines and a clear description of how you intend to use the pool or spa. The more preliminary work you do, the better off you will be.

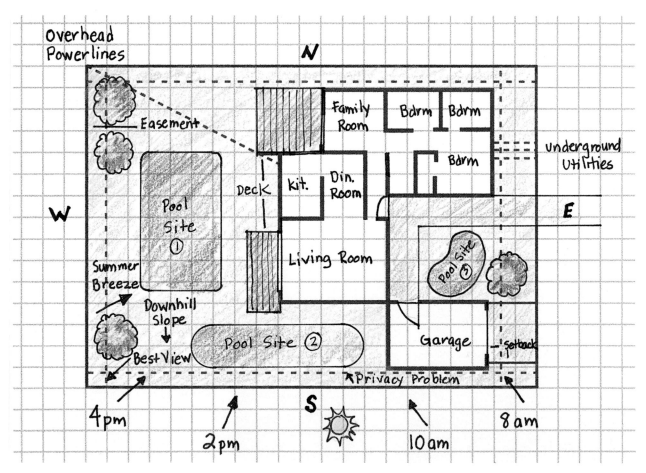

After sketching your lot and your house to scale on graph paper, you can experiment with several different pool locations. Take a look at access, as well as weather factors.

ZONING AND PERMITS

While above-ground pools and portable spas may qualify as "nonpermanent" structures that don't require local permits, large in-ground swimming pools surely do. In some municipalities, zoning ordinances govern the size and location of pools, including such things as the minimum distance to the nearest property line, as well as the required height of a safety fence. These factors can affect the placement of a swimming pool, so it is best to check in advance with your local building department. In addition, homeowner associations or restrictive covenants in your property deed may further control the possible location of a pool, and it's advisable to investigate these before making plans that will have to be changed.

If it turns out that zoning laws prohibit a pool design or location that you've selected, you may be able to file for a variance. Keep in mind, though, that this can be a lengthy and uncertain process, and it usually requires obtaining the consent of your neighbors. Contractors typically will take care of the filing for whatever permits are necessary, but a request for a variance requires the homeowner's participation.

Think of ways to use zoning requirements to stylistic advantage. The fencing shown here satisfies municipal security requirements but also lends privacy and creates a beautiful backdrop to the pool itself.

finding a professional

Once you have your basic ideas and pool possibilities firmly in mind, it will be easy to work effectively with professionals. These can include architects or designers as well as contractors. Some companies offer both design and construction services.

Because you'll have to be able to work with someone for the duration of the project—which can be many months in some cases—this is as much a search for compatible personalities as it is for expert skills and reasonable costs.

CHECKING REFERENCES

No matter how you find a contractor to interview—through an ad, a sign in front of a project, a referral from a neighbor—it's essential to check references. Ask to see a portfolio of the person's work stretching back five years or longer, and request the names of all clients during that time period. Reputable professionals will willingly give you this information. Then call several clients and ask how the project went. When you find projects similar to yours in scope and size, arrange to see them so you can judge for yourself the quality of the work. Most homeowners welcome the opportunity to help someone along and to show off their own pool or spa.

Because of the myriad choices and the engineering challenges that go into creating an elaborate pool and setting such as this one, the assistance of an architect or a professional designer is essential.

WHAT TO ASK CONTRACTORS

- Can I have a list of references that extend back for the last five years?
- Are all workers insured for workers' compensation and general liability?
- Have you worked on any projects that are similar in scope and cost to the one that I'm planning to build?
- How will cost overruns be managed? Will there be an agreed-upon price—or a pay-as-you-go arrangement?
- Who will be doing the work—the contractor or a team of subcontractors?

WHAT TO ASK FELLOW HOMEOWNERS

- Did the contractor perform the work as expected?
- Was the project completed within budget?
- Did the contractor work steadily, or were there unexplained gaps in the process?
- If there were cost overruns, were they properly explained?
- Did the contractor return promptly to make any follow-up repairs?
- If you were to do the project over again, would you use the same contractor?

SOLICITING BIDS

Ideally, several contractors will be competing for your project, but this requires that the work be spelled out in detail—including exact sizes, specific materials, and the brand names of equipment. Otherwise, estimates could vary widely because one contractor may include something that another assumed would be supplied by someone else. If you have a single contractor in mind and don't plan to get competing bids, check with neighbors, friends, and the contractor's past clients to see what they paid for similar projects.

WORKING WITH A DESIGNER

While most pool contractors can also design a standard pool, you may want something more distinctive. It might be a swimming pool with an unusual shape, a series of terraces that connect the pool with your home, or a pool house that reflects the style of your residence. Some contractors can handle these challenges alone, but in many cases a separate architect or designer will have to be brought in to help tie everything together.

Such creativity, however, comes at a cost. Some architects and designers charge a flat fee, based on the scope of the project; others charge an hourly rate, which can range anywhere from $50 to $100. Some provide construction-management services and take a percentage of the total cost as their fee.

SIGNING THE CONTRACT

Be sure to get estimates in writing, rather than over the phone. Set a reasonable deadline—a week, perhaps—to make your decision, especially if you're waiting for other bids. Don't bow to pressure from a contractor to make up your mind quickly.

The contractor best suited for the job may not necessarily be the person who gave you the lowest bid. In fact, it may be the one who submitted the highest bid, but whom you prefer based on personality, quality of work, and references. If the contractor you prefer gave you a high estimate,

it may be possible to negotiate the fee downward by showing that person the other estimates.

Once you make your choice, be sure that the contract spells out an expected start date, a completion date, and a schedule of payments. The contract should also specify that the contractor and all subcontractors agree to provide certificates of general liability insurance and workers' compensation insurance for all employees on the job. A contract is a legally binding document. Before signing it, consider having your attorney review it—to spare you any future difficulties.

Building a large in-ground swimming pool such as this one is a major construction project. Because of the high costs and lia-bilities involved, it's important to protect yourself by choosing a contractor wisely and carefully reviewing the contract.

In some cases, contractors insist on receiving a deposit when the contract is signed—but this should be no more than a token amount, and is limited in some states to $200. To protect yourself, pay for work only as it is completed, rather than up front. The final payment should be made only after the building inspector has signed off on all the work and the project is completed to your satisfaction.

Contractors should also have workers' compensation insurance for all their employees, as well as an umbrella policy that extends to subcontractors.

UNDERSTANDING LIEN WAIVERS

For a project as complicated as constructing a swimming pool, a single contractor probably will not be able to do all the work alone. Instead, independent subcontractors may perform work such as excavating the site, building decks, adding the landscaping, and installing electrical equipment.

While subcontractors are paid directly by the contractor, you should protect yourself by making sure that all the subcontractors are in fact paid for their work. Otherwise, they may try to collect any outstanding fees from you. Ask the contractor to supply a signed lien waiver from each subcontractor. This simple form certifies that the subcontractor has been paid in full for any work completed.

INSURING SUCCESS

While homeowners tend to focus on the credibility of a contractor and his or her price, another very important aspect to consider is insurance. The fact is that anyone hurt while working at your home can sue you for medical bills, lost wages, and more, unless the contractor who hires the person is adequately insured.

Ask for certificates showing proof of insurance. You should expect to see liability coverage of at least $1 million per occurrence. Request to be listed as additionally insured; your name should appear right on the insurance certificate.

planning a schedule

■ ■ ■

Although there is no standard schedule for how long it will take to build a pool, the following rough timeline can help you understand the process. The steps noted here should take place before construction begins.

12 MONTHS BEFORE THE START
Begin researching what you'd like to build by looking at magazines, other homes, and showrooms. Start creating an idea file as well as a wish list, making one column for things you must have and a separate one for things you would like.

10 TO 12 MONTHS AHEAD
Begin figuring out a budget for the pool, and consider payment possibilities—including a home equity line of credit or other loan. Also, begin asking family and friends to recommend designers and contractors.

6 TO 8 MONTHS AHEAD
Interview contractors and designers. Bring them your idea file and wish list.

2 TO 6 MONTHS AHEAD
Refine your plan to a detailed spec sheet. Solicit competitive bids or negotiate with one selected contractor if you have a preference. After choosing the contractor, decide on start and finish dates, then have an attorney look over the contract before signing it.

design options

The more you understand about the possible materials and design choices, the better you'll be able to create a pool or spa that meets your needs, at a price you can afford. Keep in mind that because contractors tend to specialize in a particular type of pool or spa, your choice of contractor will influence the overall design.

in-ground pools

In-ground pools offer the most flexibility in terms of size and style, ranging from traditional shapes to free-form fantasies. Not only can these pools be fitted into irregular lots or specific areas in your yard, they can be designed to mirror the style of your house.

A tiny pool, if well designed, can satisfy every need in terms of aesthetics and recreation.

A MATTER OF SIZE

Barring any special needs, such as a training pool for competitive swimmers or a pool large enough to handle a weekly water polo match, a backyard pool can usually be fairly small. The standard pool dimensions—20 by 40 feet, or even 15 by 30 feet—provide 450 to 800 square feet of swimming area, enough for serious exercise—or aquatic fun.

In fact, a new trend is toward pools that are smaller than 400 square feet, which can fulfill most families' demands. The advantages of smaller pools are that they can fit into the landscape more easily, they cost less to construct, and they require less money to maintain. Such "boutique pools" also have an element of intimacy that's more difficult to achieve with larger pools.

Large pools, such as this one with an elegant bowed edge, can literally fill up an entire yard and provide a spectacular space for entertaining.

The best free-form designs follow simple geometric patterns. This creative pool, for instance, is based on an octagonal shape that gives it a sense of uniformity, rather than chaos.

POOL SHAPES

Even with a modest-size pool, there are an enormous number of shape choices besides rectangles and the classic kidney design. As a rule, though, reasonably simple is best. Shapes based on rectangles, circles, and ovals won't overwhelm the landscaping. Nor will they require complicated decking or sophisticated planting schemes around them. In certain cases, though, oddly shaped pools may make the most sense—such as when you have a small, awkwardly shaped lot or want to preserve a large tree, rock outcropping, or other landscape feature.

design tip

One way to narrow the seemingly limitless possibilities for the shape of an in-ground pool is to select one that best complements the style of your house, whether traditional or contemporary, formal or casual.

55

A waterfall or fountain can be a mesmerizing addition to a pool. Water spills from a spa to a pool (left) by way of an artfully crafted basin with timeless appeal. The addition of a few boulders and some careful plantings (above) creates an altogether natural setting.

WATER FEATURES

A waterfall that spills from an in-ground spa into a pool provides a soothing and visually appealing connection between the two. Rather than an extravagance, such a water feature can be relatively inexpensive if it's built at the same time as the pool, since it will use the same pump and circulation system. The construction—which involves elevating the spa several inches above the pool, so that the water spills by gravity—is simple to engineer. However, adding a spa with a waterfall after the pool is completed is both difficult and expensive.

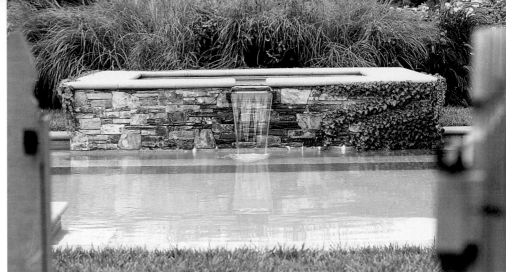

The separation between a pool and a spa offers countless opportunities for interesting water features. Here, the cascade from an ivy-covered stone spa provides an appealing focal point in the swimming pool.

Likewise, it's relatively inexpensive to integrate a fountain into the pool's pump and filtration systems during pool construction. Adding a fountain later, though, requires draining the pool, drilling through the side, and installing new plumbing (see page 169). While this can be practical if it is part of an extensive overhaul of the pool, it wouldn't be a cost-effective project on its own.

access for all

■ ■ ■

Given the therapeutic benefits of swimming, an at-home pool makes a wonderful addition for those with physical disabilities or limitations. There are several ways the physically challenged can maneuver easily and safely in and out of the water, either alone or with assistance.

With an in-ground pool, the most user-friendly solution is a ramp that leads directly from the surrounding decking into the water. It can be built at the same time as the pool, in lieu of steps. Paired with a handrail that extends up and onto the deck, such a ramp works well for those who can't navigate steps easily, and also provides access for those using an aquatic wheelchair.

Devices that can be added to an existing in-ground pool include a specially designed pool ladder with broader, closely spaced steps, and a portable ramp that extends from the deck into the water. If you're considering such a device, look for pool contractors who have experience installing them or who specialize in the design of pools for those with physical disabilities. They'll know which options are best for your circumstances.

For an above-ground pool, where a ramp isn't feasible, a comparatively low-cost option is an electronic lift, which hoists a seated person from the ground up and into the pool.

choosing materials

An in-ground pool starts with a hole in the ground similar to the kind dug for a house foundation. The hole can be lined with either concrete, vinyl, or fiberglass, which vary in cost and durability.

CONCRETE

Of all the materials available for pool construction, concrete with a plaster finish is by far the most durable. In addition to providing sheer stability, the surface is easy to replaster as needed, resulting in a pool that has a long life span.

In years past, concrete pools were built by erecting wooden forms, then pouring wet concrete into the molds, much as a house foundation is constructed. But the advent of spray-on concrete—either shotcrete or gunite—has drastically reduced the cost of construction and allowed tremendous flexibility in design.

Once the hole is excavated, the sides and the bottom are lined with a series of steel rods called rebar, which greatly increases the strength of the pool's walls and provides the elasticity needed to resist cracks. The rebar can be positioned to create nearly any shape conceivable, as well as customized steps or ramps.

Then either shotcrete or gunite is sprayed on. The two materials are very similar; the difference lies in the way they are mixed. Shotcrete is delivered to

Durability is the hallmark of concrete. A pool constructed of this material can last for generations.

the site already mixed, and is then mixed further with air and sprayed onto the rebar with a hose. Gunite is delivered in a dry form, then mixed with both water and air as it is sprayed into place. Because it can be mixed at the

site as it's needed, gunite is more popular than shotcrete, but they produce identical linings when applied correctly.

Not only does this spray-on technology give a contractor absolute freedom in determining the size and shape of a concrete swimming pool, but in most cases the price is based on the pool's perimeter. That means that a pool with contemporary curves will cost no more than the same size pool with traditional right angles.

More than just durable, concrete is also the most versatile material for pool construction. Its shape is limited only by the imagination of the designer who puts a pencil to paper, or the contractor who sets to work with a shovel.

VINYL

The advent of vinyl for lining in-ground pools has produced a surge in construction, because of both the lower cost (see page 34) and the easier installation compared to shotcrete or gunite. Instead of requiring a month or more, building a vinyl-lined pool usually can be completed in a matter of days.

Vinyl pools are actually a combination of a large, flexible container—the liner—and supporting walls made of aluminum, steel, plastic, masonry block, or even wood. The bottom of the liner rests on a bed of flattened sand or other material, while its

Even though they're prefabricated, vinyl pools are available in a range of shapes and sizes. A vinyl pool is much quicker to install than one made of concrete.

comparison of materials

TYPE	COST	EASE OF PROJECT	LONGEVITY
Concrete (shotcrete or gunite)	high	complex	excellent
Fiberglass	high	simple	good
Vinyl	low	moderate	good

top is secured by special material called coping that creates a finished edge to the pool and serves as a border for the deck. Vinyl-lined pools are manufactured in dozens of different styles, sizes, and colors, so although customizing isn't possible, most homeowners will find a satisfactory option.

Vinyl deteriorates over time as a result of exposure to ultraviolet radiation and to pool chemicals. Typically, a vinyl liner will last 10 to 12 years. To prevent fading

and staining, some liners include ultraviolet and fungus inhibitors, which extend the life of the liner to 18 or 20 years. In many cases, replacing the liner is a straightforward matter—although doing so will most likely cost between $5,000 and $10,000. But if the pool is built in clay soil, which expands when wet, the liner can't be replaced easily. If this is your situation, you'll have to excavate again and completely rebuild the pool.

FIBERGLASS

For ease of in-ground pool construction, nothing can match fiberglass. Be aware, though, that it may be more expensive than concrete and is certainly not as long-lasting.

A fiberglass swimming pool is sold as a gigantic one-piece shell that is brought to your home by truck and set in place in an excavated hole with the use of a crane. Then the plumbing and electrical systems are connected to the outside wall.

Because fiberglass pools are purchased ready-made, it is not possible to request a customized design—but most manufacturers offer dozens of models and sizes to choose from, complete with pre-formed steps, spas, and benches.

In years past, the quality of fiberglass pools was far inferior to the alternatives, leading to problems such as leaks and buckling. Advances in technology, however, have largely eliminated these weaknesses. But the sheer size of such pools limits their availability because it is quite expensive to truck them over great distances.

The basic form of a fiberglass pool is made on an upside-down mold. Then a coating is applied to create a smooth inside surface. This slick surface is difficult for algae to cling to, making it easy to keep a fiberglass pool clean. But

A fiberglass pool—even an extremely large one—arrives at the site ready-made and is then carefully positioned in the excavated hole.

over 10 to 15 years, the combined forces of sunlight and pool chemicals begin to deteriorate the surface and turn it slightly chalky. Recoating it is tricky and not always successful because the new coating does not adhere easily to the old one. In addition, recoating a fiberglass pool requires that it be completely drained, which can present problems: since the pool itself does not offer much structural support, draining may cause cave-ins if the pool has been constructed in an expansive soil such as clay.

above-ground pools

While not as luxurious as in-ground pools, above-ground pools have their distinct advantages. They're inexpensive and easy to install. Because they are classified as nonpermanent structures, adding one does not usually require a building permit and will not trigger an increase in real estate taxes.

A POOL ON THE GO

If you envision a pool as a permanent addition to your home, an in-ground pool makes the best sense from an investment perspective. But an above-ground pool can be disassembled and transported in a moving van, making it a popular choice for renters or for those who are planning a move sometime soon. It's also a good option if you want a pool just for a few years while your children are young.

POOLS IN AN INSTANT

All of the hassles of constructing an in-ground pool—from getting building permits to having major earth-moving equipment rumbling through the backyard—vanish with above-ground models. Above-ground pools require little or no excavation, cost a fraction of the price of an in-ground pool, and can even be installed by a savvy do-it-yourself homeowner, which

With astute planning, an above-ground pool can become an enticing element in a yard. Here, a sloping site makes it possible to build a deck around part of the pool—which gives it a built-in look.

will further reduce costs. It's no wonder that more above-ground pools are sold each year than in-ground ones.

For all its ease, though, a portable pool can be difficult to assemble correctly. Unless it's small or extremely simple, installing it will most likely require the help of a swimming pool dealer (see more about installation on pages 122 to 125).

MATERIALS

Unlike the great variety of materials, styles, and construction techniques available for in-ground pools, above-ground pools tend to have more uniformity. In general, these pools sit directly on the ground and require no excavation other than simple grading to create a flat surface. Most have a constant depth throughout—usually about 4 feet—although shapes can vary from rectangular to circular. In most cases, above-ground pools contain vinyl liners that are held in place by self-supporting walls made of galvanized steel, plastic, or aluminum.

Creative landscaping makes an above-ground pool every bit as beautiful as one of its more expensive cousins. A richness of hedges and tiered plantings cleverly conceals this pool's humble design.

SITING AN ABOVE-GROUND POOL

These versatile pools can be set up in a wide variety of sites, usually requiring only a flat surface and reasonable access. Be sure to follow the same guidelines as for an in-ground pool (pages 38 to 39). Although above-ground pools are called portable, you definitely won't want to have to disassemble yours and move it after it's situated.

CREATING A PERMANENT LOOK

Above-ground swimming pools benefit greatly from simple additions that make them seem more at home in a yard. This might be fencing that conceals the pool's underpinnings from view or a basic deck. In many cases, the pool kit itself contains decking, ranging from a small sitting area on one side to a surface that surrounds the entire pool and is wide enough for furniture and entertaining.

If your pool kit doesn't contain decking, it's possible to build a deck separately. This works especially well if you can site the pool on a flat surface a few feet lower than the house. Then the deck can connect from the house directly to the top of the swimming pool, creating the illusion of an in-ground pool.

FINDING A REPUTABLE DEALER

Quality and warranties vary widely for above-ground pools, even more widely than for in-ground ones. Advertisements often lure shoppers with offers of low prices, but the chances of ending up with an inferior product when shopping by price alone are great. Here's how to ensure that the above-ground pool you choose will last:

- Ask the dealer for the names and telephone numbers of customers from the past several years, not just the past season. Call them up and visit as many of the pools as you can in person to make sure the quality is what you expect. The goal is to see how the pools hold up over time, rather than how inviting they look a month after installation.

- Read product reviews of the various pools you are considering, either in consumer magazines or through an Internet search. Often, various models produced by different manufacturers will look identical, but some will be far more durable than others for the same price.

- Make sure you understand the warranty, as well as the dealer's ability to remedy any problems that may arise. Be wary of warranties that cover only parts and materials and not the labor required to install them. In most cases, the charge for parts is very little compared to the cost of having them replaced.

Here, the focus is on the elaborate decking and plantings, which serve to enhance the overall appeal of the modest pool.

an enclosed pool

A pool inside an enclosure offers an enormous advantage over one that's exposed to the elements: the option of swimming year-round no matter what the weather. To have a pool that's protected, you can either construct one indoors or enclose an outdoor pool.

BUILDING A POOL INDOORS

Most often, constructing an indoor pool will involve adding on to your house. It's important to follow the usual guidelines for an addition—consulting an architect, hiring a contractor, and so forth. The pool's location is crucial. Of course, you'll want to avoid accessing it via a formal living room or a dining room. You may want to site it near a bathroom or another room with a non-carpeted floor. More important, you'll need to deal with the issues of chemical odors and humidity.

While the odor of a pool throughout the house can simply be annoying, the humidity that builds up can cause serious problems such as mold and rot. To prevent this, you'll need to build a true separation between the house and the pool, in the form of a corridor or doors that prevent the transfer of odors and humidity.

In addition, the pool area will need adequate ventilation so that the vapors can be transferred outdoors. The ideal ventilation system will depend on the size of the pool, the dimensions of the enclosure, and the average temperature of the pool area. When choosing a contractor, be sure to enlist one who has past experience building indoor pools—and visit several of his or her previous projects to check their conditions, preferably after the pool has been in use for several years.

Part atrium, part recreation center, an enclosed swimming pool can offer a year-round retreat from stress.

ENCLOSING AN OUTDOOR POOL

Enclosures for pools range in materials and design from simple to luxurious. Among the simplest designs are geodesic domes that are fitted inexpensively over existing pools. They extend the swimming season by trapping heat in the manner of a greenhouse. In most cases, domes are removed during the summer, when they tend to overheat the pool. Another low-cost option is an air-inflated canopy. Although canopies are noisy—because of the required air blower—and fairly delicate, they are easy to add and remove.

More elaborate enclosures resemble greenhouse conservatories. Permanent structures with glass panels and roofs, they provide a year-round swimming and entertaining environment, complete with heating and cooling systems for maximum comfort. The cost of these enclosures can far exceed the cost of the pool itself, since they are equivalent to a house in terms of the mechanical systems that run them and the level of finish work needed to complete them.

For financial reasons, you may decide to build an outdoor pool now and defer adding an enclosure to it until sometime in the future.

Outdoor conservatory-style enclosures extend the swimming season and keep away insects.

In that case, be sure to locate mechanical equipment wisely, so that it won't interfere with the placement of the enclosure. If the enclosure you're planning requires a foundation, you can save money by building it during the construction of the pool, when the excavation equipment is already on site.

smart tip

Because an indoor pool is as permanent a structure as a house, it makes sense to select materials that will last as long as a house would. The best choice is a pool made of gunite or shotcrete, rather than a fiberglass pool or one lined with vinyl.

underwater lighting

If a pool or spa is to be used in the evening, proper lighting is essential for safety. But beyond making it easier to navigate in the dark, lighting also creates an opportunity to add interesting accents to the pool. In the past, all lighting had to be added during construction—and incandescent lighting still must be put in at that time. Fiber-optic technology, however, has created do-it-yourself possibilities for an existing pool.

When properly conceived, lighting is as much a part of the pool landscape as decking and plantings.

INCANDESCENT LIGHTING

Safety considerations may incline you toward incandescent lighting, which provides strong illumination. To eliminate the risk of shock that results from combining electrical connections with water, these lights come completely sealed inside a protective waterproof niche.

But since the bulbs are sealed as well as the fixtures, changing them when they burn out requires a little extra effort. You literally pull the light out of the pool wall on its specially designed extension cord, bringing it to the surface, where you replace the burnt-out bulb. You then reposition the entire apparatus in the waterproof niche.

Due to the engineering involved in constructing an underwater lighting system and the difficulty of wiring a pool, these lights need to be installed when the pool is built—they are nearly impossible to install afterward.

A long cord allows removal of underwater lights when it's time to replace a bulb.

FIBER-OPTIC LIGHTING

With this type of lighting, a cord carries light, rather than electricity, to the pool. A lens at the end of the cord releases the illumination, eliminating any electrical hazards. Because the electric source lies outside the pool, fiber-optic lights are ideal for adding to an existing pool. A knowledgeable homeowner can safely and easily do the job without a contractor.

Fiber-optic lighting tends to be far more subtle than the incandescent variety, creating many aesthetic possibilities for accent lighting, both within the pool and just beneath the coping that encircles it. Resist the temptation to add too many fiber-optic lights; the result can be a chaotic nighttime scene. Add lights sparingly to create a simple effect, rather than a dazzling light show.

A combination of lighting—from underwater to fiber-optic to ordinary incandescent—can be used to give a swimming pool and spa an other-worldly aura.

design tip

The services of a lighting designer are often available free of charge when you purchase lighting, so take advantage of a professional's expertise.

understanding spas

The term "spa" refers to any small pool that contains benches for seating, jets to whirl the water into a tension-releasing froth of bubbles, and a heater to keep the water bathtub warm. The design choices are vast, including integral spas connected directly to swimming pools, portable spas that can be set up anywhere indoors or out, and traditional hot tubs that can be made of wood or other materials and may or may not have churning action.

IN-GROUND SPAS

For those who already have a swimming pool or are building one, the easiest way to create a spa is to build one right into the pool. The spa can be made of the same materials as the pool, and connected to the same water supply and filtration systems. You can also save considerably on heating costs, since the water may already be heated in the pool. Even if the swimming pool is closed off for the winter, it is possible to use the spa portion year-round, although you may need to take extra steps to protect plumbing systems from freezing (see page 199).

Those without a swimming pool can build a spa directly into the ground in the manner of a miniature swimming pool, which is how spas were originally built. However, the expense of this sort of construction has made this choice unpopular. Because of the extensive plumbing and electrical systems involved, a stand-alone in-ground spa can cost nearly two-thirds the amount of a full-sized swimming pool.

Raising the spa above the level of the adjoining pool makes a bold architectural statement that heightens the effectiveness of this design.

A loose grouping of boulders and river rocks helps this spa blend into its natural surroundings.

For an indoor spa to work well, location is crucial. Here a brick floor provides a water-friendly surface, while a collection of house-plants and a view to the outdoors create an inviting setting.

An insulating cover saves energy and keeps the water of this nicely sited above-ground spa clean.

PORTABLE SPAS

A newer addition to the world of spas and hot tubs is the portable spa. The plumbing and electrical systems come completely assembled in these units and the filtration system is self-contained, which makes them easy to set up either indoors or out. They generally require no building permit and will not raise property taxes since they are not permanent structures. Sizes vary widely, from small 125-gallon versions that seat two to larger 500-gallon styles that seat eight.

Some portable spas run on standard 120-volt current, so they can be plugged into any outlet. Others run on 240-volt current, similar to electric dryers. Although the latter need to be connected by an electrician, they have greater heating capacity, and the jets can be used in combination with heaters.

A portable spa on a patio, complete with a view toward the distant water, requires only minimum effort to set up and maintain.

74

CLASSIC HOT TUBS

Usually made of wood such as rot-resistant redwood or red cedar, these spas are built like giant barrels, with staves of wood held together by steel hoops. As the staves swell with water, they form a leakproof seal, and a perfect—and picturesque—tub. Classic hot tubs can be fitted with jets to create whirlpool action, or left as still pools with just the action of the filter to keep the water moving.

These wooden tubs have suffered in reputation in recent years, mostly because wood is not as sanitary as other surfaces. But they can be fitted with a vinyl liner, which eliminates the hygiene problem. Paying careful attention to the water filtration and chemistry will also keep a classic tub fresh and viable (see pages 176 to 185).

CHOOSING THE RIGHT SPA

Spas, like cars, come in a huge variety of both styles and quality. The market is saturated with cheap portable spas that may not hold up. To make sure you choose a spa that lasts, avoid impulse shopping. Research the specific brands you're considering by looking up product reviews on the Internet, asking friends and family for their recommendations, and spending time at spa dealers testing out their various models. Large dealers have working display models in their showrooms that you can try on the spot. Be sure to bring your bathing suit!

A classic wooden hot tub has a nostalgic beauty all its own.

a spa to swim in

∎ ∎ ∎

A swim spa combines the compact size of a spa with the exercise possibilities of a pool. Most swim spas are 13 to 15 feet long and 6 to 8 feet wide—far smaller than a swimming pool, yet easily twice the length of a standard spa.

Strong jets create a swirling current to swim against, allowing you to get a workout by swimming in place. The water is usually kept cooler than in a spa, since exercising in warm water can be exhausting, but the temperature can easily be raised for a hotter soak. In some models, a removable partition makes it possible to heat a small portion of the spa for soaking, while leaving the remainder at a cooler temperature for swimming.

One word of warning: not all swimmers enjoy using a swim spa, which is the aquatic equivalent of running on a treadmill. Before purchasing one, be sure to try it out at a dealer's showroom.

pool and spa equipment

What's the most appealing feature of a pool or spa? For most people, it's clear, sparkling water at the perfect temperature. Achieving this inviting state depends in part on managing the water chemistry—discussed on pages 176 to 185—but the pool or spa's mechanical equipment plays a big role as well. Understanding that system, which circulates, filters, and warms the water, will help you make efficient, cost-effective choices.

water works

Water in a swimming pool, whether above-ground or in-ground, needs to circulate in order to stay fresh. Circulation accomplishes several things. It helps mix chemicals in the water and dilute heated water evenly to prevent warm spots and cold spots. Most important, it makes it possible to strain and filter out any debris or particulates in the water.

SWIMMING POOL PIPES AND PLUMBING

Just behind the walls and underneath the deck of an in-ground swimming pool—or attached to the outside wall of an above-ground pool—lies a network of pipes that rivals a home's plumbing system in complexity.

The water within a pool's support system flows under pressure in a continuous loop. Water drains from the pool, either through the main drain or through side drains called skimmers. Next it passes through a pump that pressurizes it, forcing it through a filter and a heater (if the pool has one). From there, the water travels through return lines and sprays back into the pool through nozzles known as inlets.

A complicated network of plumbing keeps the water circulating in a pool or spa so that it can be filtered and heated.

A pool's plumbing system is the essential element in keeping water clean.

money-saving tip

In a house, the best-quality pipes for delivering water are made of copper. Not so in a pool. Because this water is not for drinking, plastic pipes made from PVC or the similar CPVC are perfectly safe and offer several advantages. They're inexpensive, easy to work with, and—most important—resistant to corrosion.

BEHIND THE SCENES OF A SWIMMING POOL

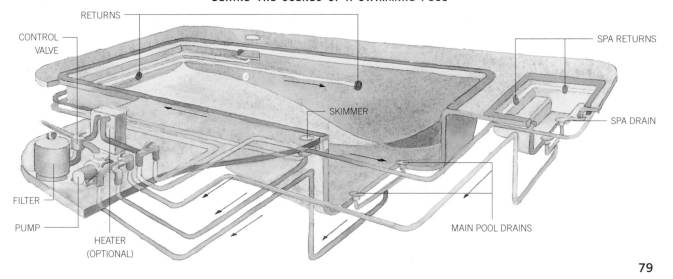

CONTROL VALVE

RETURNS

SPA RETURNS

SPA DRAIN

SKIMMER

FILTER

PUMP

HEATER (OPTIONAL)

MAIN POOL DRAINS

skimmers, drains, and inlets

Skimmers and drains draw water into the pump and the filtration system, then inlets return clean water back into the pool. Here's how these devices work together.

SURFACE SKIMMERS

As their name suggests, these devices help keep pools clean by skimming water and capturing any floating debris, such as leaves and grass clippings. Essentially, they do the same job as gutters do in large commercial swimming pools. They're built into the upper sides of an in-ground pool, where their suction action draws in pool litter and traps it. Convenient access permits the trapped debris to be emptied easily. Skimmers also create an opening for attaching a portable aquatic vacuum. The vacuum's tube connects to the skimmer's suction line and is powered by the pool pump.

A typical surface skimmer is made of precast concrete or plastic and consists of a tank with a projecting throat on its upper side (see the illustration below). A self-adjusting piece of plastic, called a weir, performs the skimming action by regulating the amount of water that enters the skimmer. Because the weir adjusts to allow only a thin layer of water to spill over, water is pulled off the surface rapidly—effectively keeping a large area of the pool surface clear.

In general, one well-located skimmer can keep up to 500 square feet of pool surface clean. However, if the debris that's gathered by a skimmer is left to accumulate, it will put extra strain on the pump. For best results, the skimmer basket should be cleaned out each day.

Skimmers must be installed with an equalizer line—a pipe that connects from the bottom of the skimmer basket through the pool wall and into the water. The equalizer prevents air from being sucked into the system if evaporation causes the water level to drop below the level of the weir. If air were to enter the system, it would cause the pump to stall.

ABOVE-GROUND POOL SKIMMERS

Because above-ground pools have thin walls, it is not possible to place skimmer baskets within them. Instead, special collector units that hang on the side of the pool or float in the water can be attached to the pump mechanism to provide effective skimming action (see the illustration at right). One drawback, however, is that these units project into the pool instead of lying flush with the wall, creating a swimming obstacle. The hand skimmer is a labor-intensive alternative. It's simply a large net that you pass over the water surface each day to catch and remove debris.

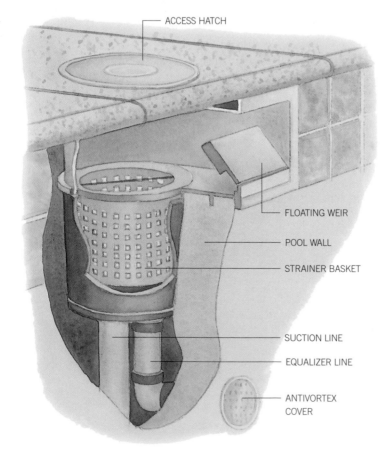

ACCESS HATCH

FLOATING WEIR

POOL WALL

STRAINER BASKET

SUCTION LINE

EQUALIZER LINE

ANTIVORTEX COVER

Crystal-clear water is the key ingredient of a beautiful pool, as in this pristine in-ground example. To keep the surface free of debris, the strainer baskets should be cleaned regularly.

FLOATING SKIMMER FOR ABOVE-GROUND POOL

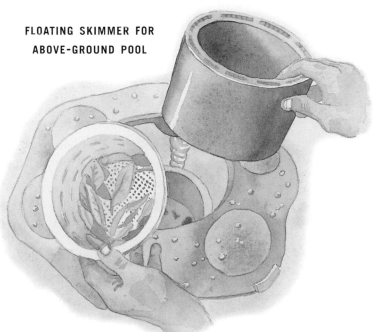

quick tip

Skimmers are most effective when located on the downwind side of the pool, since wind will push debris toward the opening.

DRAINS

In addition to skimmers, most pools have a pair of main drains at the bottom, usually situated in the deepest point in the pool, with the entire floor slanting toward them. Debris, which naturally settles to the lowest area, is sucked automatically through the main drains toward the pump, then through the filter.

THE ANTIVORTEX COVER If you've ever placed your hand over the main drain in a swimming pool, you've felt the tug generated by the pump. In pools with two drains and multiple skimmer baskets, having one blocked drain will not create a dangerous situation. But where there is only one drain, a blocked flow can create a hazardous form of suction known as a vortex. This strong pull can trap swimmers even in a shallow pool, posing a grave danger. Having multiple drains and skimmers reduces the risk but doesn't eliminate it.

To further enhance safety, all drains—as well as all equalizers installed with skimmers—should be fitted with an antivortex cover. This slatted or perforated cover, similar to a drain cover in a shower, prevents hair and limbs from becoming caught in the plumbing. If antivortex covers are in place and the pool is built and operated correctly, there is virtually no risk of suction pinning someone against a drain.

THE HYDROSTATIC VALVE Groundwater that lies beneath the swimming pool is not a problem as long as the pool is filled; the sheer weight of the water keeps the pool structure firmly in place. If the pool is emptied, however, groundwater exerts tremendous pressure against the bottom and sides of the pool. This pressure can be so great that it cracks concrete pools and causes fiberglass pools to lift up out of the ground.

Fitting each main drain with a hydrostatic relief valve prevents the problem. The valve consists of a floating ball that lies in a pipe

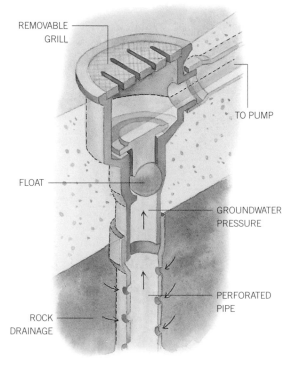

REMOVABLE GRILL

TO PUMP

FLOAT

GROUNDWATER PRESSURE

PERFORATED PIPE

ROCK DRAINAGE

Drains are required in all pools and spas—not just to empty water periodically but to draw water into the filter. A hydrostatic valve in the main drain (left) allows groundwater to flow into an emptied pool, which prevents the shell from cracking or heaving out of the ground.

between the drain and the groundwater. During normal operation, the water in the pool presses down against the ball and seals the drain off from the groundwater. When the pool is empty, however, the ball floats up and unblocks the pipe if the pressure from the groundwater increases to dangerous levels. Then, instead of cracking or lifting, the pool simply fills with harmless groundwater.

INLETS

Once water passes through the pump, it returns to the pool via the inlets. Rather than just allowing water to run back into the pool, inlets focus and concentrate the flow, jetting the water into the pool. This process helps distribute chemicals evenly and mixes heated water with cooler water to provide a uniform temperature.

pumps

Like the body's heart, the electric pump in a swimming pool forms the mechanical center of the water circulation system. In a typical pump, an electric motor spins a blade that is known as an impeller—similar to a propeller—located inside the pump housing. The impeller drives water from the various pool drains through the filter, then back out into the pool through the inlets.

PUMP CAPACITY

In general, a pump should be able to circulate the entire volume of water in the pool at least once every 24 hours—and once every 8 hours is preferable to guarantee cleanliness. (The required circulation rate is often governed by local building codes, so check with your building department for specifics.) The volume of water flow depends on the diameter of the pipes in the plumbing system and the size of the motor powering the pump.

PIPE DIAMETER Most commonly, pipes that drain the pool measure 2 inches in diameter. Return pipes typically start at $1\frac{1}{2}$ inches but connect to smaller pipes of $\frac{3}{4}$ or even $\frac{1}{2}$ inch where they reach the

Pumps vary in size according to the amount of water they have to circulate. A properly sized pump should be able to turn over the entire volume of water once every 8 to 24 hours.

inlets. This decrease in size increases the pressure, creating jets of water that help distribute chemicals and heat evenly.

MOTOR SIZE Usually, a 1.5-horse-power pump is sufficient. Many pool owners assume that a larger motor will move the water faster, but that isn't true—the flow of water is limited by the size of the pipes, so a larger pump will be working in vain to force water out faster. This puts it under heavy strain, which will seriously shorten its life: a properly sized pump might last 10 years or longer, but an oversized pump being strained might burn out after only three or four years. Also, an overworked pump is noisy. Matching the pump to the plumbing system requires careful calculation and is best left to a contractor.

WATER OUTLET

WATER INLET

MOTOR

STRAINER BASKET

IMPELLER

Two-speed pumps are often used for spas. The higher speed is used to power the hydrojets; the lower speed operates the circulation through the filter and heater—and saves energy when the spa is not in use.

money-saving tip

For maximum efficiency, the pump should be installed no farther than 40 to 60 feet from the pool. Any farther than that will necessitate an increase in pump horsepower or the addition of a secondary booster pump to help send water back into the pool. Either way, it will add to the noise and to the expense.

filters

While the pool's skimmer basket removes floating debris, the filtration system removes the nearly invisible particles that cause water to appear cloudy. Ordinary filtration systems do not remove bacteria, however, which is why chemical treatment is required as well (see pages 176 to 185). Even so, a well-functioning filter is an essential element in maintaining water clarity.

Maintaining the filter of a pool or spa keeps the water fresh and inviting through the entire swimming season.

CHOOSING THE RIGHT FILTER

Filters come in an array of possibilities. There are high-rate sand filters, filters filled with pulverized material called diatomaceous earth, and cartridge filters, which are similar to the air filter in a car in both convenience and effectiveness. In the past, all three were viable choices for residential pools, but recent advances in cartridge filters have made them overwhelmingly preferred—about 99 percent of pool owners use a cartridge filter. A look at all the options will help explain why.

HIGH-RATE SAND FILTERS

Until recently, the high-rate sand filter was the most popular option for swimming pools. These filters contain pressurized tanks built of fiberglass, stainless steel, or plastic and are filled with special grades of sand that can trap particles as small as 5 microns (the typical human hair follicle measures between 40 and 120 microns thick). Water enters from the top, is forced to a drain at the bottom, then feeds back into the swimming pool. The pressurized system drives particles in the water deep into the sand bed.

The drawback of these filters is that the sand they contain must be backwashed frequently in order to remove the particles and increase the efficiency of the filtering medium. While not a difficult task, backwashing does use a great deal of water—as much as 500 gallons per cleaning.

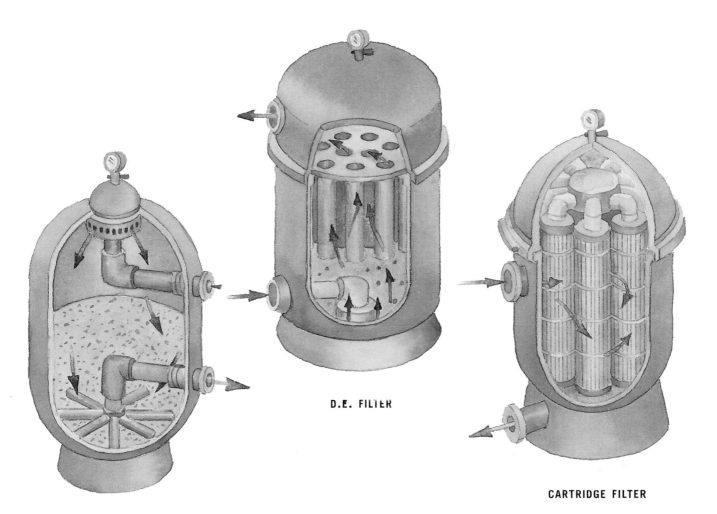

SAND FILTER

D.E. FILTER

CARTRIDGE FILTER

DIATOMACEOUS EARTH (D.E.) FILTERS

In these filters, water from the pool passes through filter grids coated with diatomaceous earth, a fine powder made from the chemically inert, fossilized remains of sea organisms called diatoms. Particles in the water catch on the edges of the D.E. and are held tight. D.E. filters are more compact than high-rate sand filters, since they do not contain a pressurized tank. More important, they filter out tinier particles—as small as 3 microns in diameter.

But while these filters are effective, they also require backwashing, which again means using as much as 500 gallons of water each time. Worse, the diatomaceous earth itself is classified as a hazardous waste in many localities, and disposal is increasingly regulated.

CARTRIDGE FILTERS

Commercial and public swimming pools require high-rate sand or D.E. filters because they can clean very small particles out of the water. For residential pools, however, the best choice is a cartridge filter.

The latest cartridge filters are almost as effective as high-rate sand filters, trapping particles as small as 6 microns. They're also much easier and safer to maintain, and require very little water for cleaning.

In a cartridge filter, pool water passes through a filter made of polyester cloth or corrugated paper. Instead of backwashing, you simply remove the filter and hose it off. After a few years, the filter will need replacing, but this is a simple process explained in the manufacturer's instructions.

heaters

Delightful as a pool looks, it's how swimming in it feels that makes the more lasting impression—and that means having a comfortable water temperature. The ideal temperature depends on your personal preference, but the range is usually between 78 and 82 degrees. Even in summer, the only way to guarantee that warmth is with a heater.

CHOOSING A HEATER

Pool heaters come in a number of styles based on the energy source they use. The cost to run the different types of heaters also varies widely, depending on the region you live in. Electricity, for instance, is far cheaper in some areas than in others. An experienced pool contractor will know which type of heater is the best value for your region.

GAS HEATERS

Gas heaters are the most popular type of pool heater because of the relatively low cost of the fuel. In addition, they're convenient and tend to heat water quickly because they use a direct flame. Gas heaters run on either propane or natural gas, and are divided into three distinct types.

COIL GAS HEATER

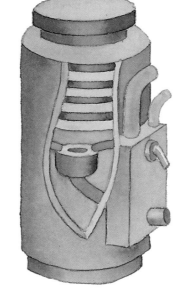

CONVECTION HEATER

CONVECTION HEATERS A large flame heats a steady stream of slow-moving water to a very high temperature. This type of heater is suitable for small pools and spas.

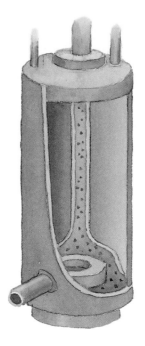

TANK HEATER

TANK HEATERS A small flame heats a large volume of water; it's cost-effective, but not sufficient in cold climates.

COIL, OR FLASH, HEATERS This is the most common type of gas heater. A large flame rapidly heats a coil through which a small but fast-moving stream of water passes.

Although the most expensive type of heater to use since they consume the largest quantity of fuel, coil heaters are suited for pools and spas of any size because they heat a large body of water quickly.

COIL HEATER

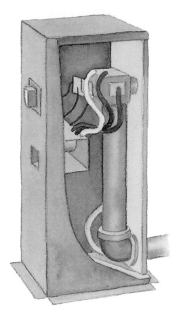

ELECTRIC HEATER

ELECTRIC HEATERS

Electric heaters, similar to those used for electric hot-water tanks in homes, heat water by emitting an electric current that produces heat in a coil. The coil warms a tank of water, a fairly slow process. While the purchase price of an electric heater is slightly less than that of a propane or natural gas heater, the cost of electricity in most parts of the country makes these heaters the most expensive to use—and a poor choice.

ELECTRIC HEAT PUMPS

One way electricity *can* be used wisely to heat a pool is to connect a water heater to a heat pump. Heat pumps operate on the same principle as air conditioners: refrigerants, heat exchangers, and compressors combine to transfer heat from one area to another rather than to generate heat.

But while an air conditioner transfers heat from inside to outside, a heat pump in a pool transfers heat from the air to the water. Warm outside air heats the refrigerant within the heat pump; it is then further heated and compressed by the compressor, resulting in a very hot gas. When the gas passes through a heat exchanger, its heat is transferred to the pool water.

The beauty of a heat pump is that although it runs on electricity, it actually yields many times more heat than could be produced by the same amount of electricity running an electric heater alone. The downside is that heat pumps work best in hot climates and are of little use in warming a pool in a northern climate during the spring and fall.

ELECTRIC HEAT PUMP

ELECTRIC HEATER

smart tip

Because a heater is connected to the plumbing outside the pool, rather than to the piping installed within the pool, it is very easy to add a heater after the pool is built. If you're thinking of adding a heater some time in the future, have all the necessary plumbing installed ahead of time.

Even in a woodsy location, wisely sited solar panels can result in substantial savings in the cost of heating a pool.

smart tip

When installing solar collectors or combination systems, always choose a contractor who has a lengthy track record working with solar heat. While many contractors may think they can manage the simple technology, solar components require careful installation that only someone with experience should tackle. Choosing the right contractor will help avoid expensive mistakes.

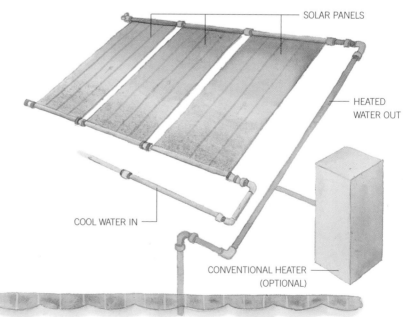

SOLAR PANELS

HEATED WATER OUT

COOL WATER IN

CONVENTIONAL HEATER (OPTIONAL)

GOING SOLAR

Because of the big expense of heating pool water, solar energy is an increasingly appealing option. The single best way to ensure being able to trap solar energy is to site the pool well. If the pool has full southern or southwesterly exposure, with no shade from trees, then the water will heat up on its own, sometimes eliminating the need for supplemental heating entirely, but in any case reducing heating costs.

USING SOLAR COLLECTORS

If more heat is needed than what the pool water alone can absorb, you can add solar collectors elsewhere. These devices are constructed simply and consist of a black metal plate with water-filled tubes running through it; the tubes are covered with clear acrylic to prevent loss of heat from wind. Pool water is warmed when the metal plate absorbs heat from the sun and transfers it to the water in the tubes, which flows back into the pool.

As a general rule, the surface area of solar collectors must add up to at least 75 percent of the surface area of the pool; for example, if the swimming pool has a surface area of 400 square feet, a total of 300 square feet of collectors is needed. Solar collectors can be positioned anywhere on the property, but the most common location is on the roof of the house, facing directly south or slightly to the southwest.

A COMBINATION SYSTEM

Not all locations are ideally suited to using solar collectors, both because of the number of collectors needed and because the exposure has to be right. In addition, solar collectors do not work well in colder climates in the wintertime, for obvious reasons. Still, it is possible to produce at least some heat from solar collectors in many areas. A combination system will enable you to partially warm water through collectors, then warm it further with a conventional heater, reducing your overall heating bill.

WHAT SIZE HEATER?

The heating capacity of gas heaters is measured in British Thermal Units, or BTUs. A single BTU is defined as the amount of heat needed to raise the temperature of 1 pound of water 1 degree Fahrenheit. The range of pool heaters goes from 20,000 BTUs to 200,000 BTUs and beyond. The size heater you will need will depend on your geographic location as well as how the pool will be used. If the goal is to add a few degrees of extra heat during the peak summer swim season, a small heater will suffice—possibly one that produces fewer than 50,000 BTUs. But if you want to extend the swim season year-round, you'll need a more powerful heater.

While calculations based on pool volume and the relative day- and nighttime temperature averages can produce a BTU requirement, there are too many other variables, including wind conditions and water-cooling evaporation, to give you an exact number for your situation. It makes better sense to rely on the advice of an experienced contractor as well as to talk to friends and neighbors in order to arrive at a realistic heater capacity.

calculating pool volume
■ ■ ■

To select an appropriate heater, it's essential to know the volume of water in your pool. If your contractor cannot give you this information, you can estimate the number of gallons yourself. For a rectangular pool, multiply the length by the width by the average depth to determine the number of cubic feet. For a free-form pool, you may have to estimate the length and width, or break the pool into smaller segments and calculate each separately.

Once you have the volume in cubic feet, multiply that number by 7.48 (the number of gallons in 1 cubic foot of water) to yield the number of gallons in your pool. For example, a rectangular pool that is 20 by 40 feet and averages 6 feet deep will contain 4,800 cubic feet of water. This translates to more than 35,000 gallons of water.

housing the equipment

Pool equipment—including the pump, filter, and heater—is built largely from plastic and other noncorrosive materials, allowing it to be placed out in the open and withstand the elements year-round. In most cases, all that is needed is a simple concrete pad for the equipment to rest on. However, pool owners often want to hide the equipment from view.

This can be accomplished by shielding it behind a section of fencing, a simple hedge, or a small stand of evergreen trees or shrubs. Or the pool equipment can be housed in a separate shed, situated beneath a deck, or hidden from view entirely in an equipment room attached to a pool house or cabana. In addition to making the surroundings more pleasant, concealing the equipment can also help reduce noise from the pump.

safety tip

If you're planning to house the plumbing, filtering, and heating equipment in one section of a pool house or cabana, proper ventilation is essential for a heater fueled with gas or propane. Ventilation will ensure that no fumes, in particular deadly carbon monoxide, can accumulate. To do the job right, have an experienced contractor set up the equipment, and be sure to install carbon monoxide detectors that sound an alert if there's a problem.

Properly situated, a pool house or cabana can help conceal equipment and muffle sounds.

This small cedar building houses the mechanical equipment for an in-ground pool and spa. In addition to hiding equipment from view, the shed protects it from the weather and provides storage for chemicals and tools.

Part of the attraction of this in-ground spa is its simplicity, with no equipment in sight. The wooden deck covers the spa workings, which can be accessed easily by opening a hinged hatch.

Above-ground pools naturally create niches to hide pool equipment. Here, the machinery is tucked beneath the pool's raised deck and is blocked from view by a wooden gate that latches into place.

pool covers

Of all the accessories that can be added to a swimming pool, a cover makes the most practical sense. First, it keeps debris as well as rainwater and snowmelt out of the pool—which greatly eases maintenance as well as the load on the pump and filter. Second, by reducing heat loss from evaporation and heat radiation, a cover can lower heating bills substantially. Finally, a specially designed pool cover can act as a safety device by supporting the weight of a person who falls on or walks across it.

COVERS FOR EASY MAINTENANCE

The simplest pool cover amounts to little more than a giant tarp that is stretched over the surface of an above-ground or in-ground pool. Such covers need to be firmly attached along the edges so they don't blow away in the wind. Special ties will anchor them, or the edges can be weighted down with sand- or water-filled bags. Many of the simplest covers are loose fitting. To prevent rainwater and snow from weighing them down, add a floating ball beneath the cover, which will prevent precipitation from pooling. For maximum protection, make sure the cover extends at least 5 feet beyond the edge of an in-ground pool.

COVERS FOR ENERGY EFFICIENCY

During swimming season, a pool tends to gain heat from the sun during the day, then lose it at night through heat radiation as well as evaporation. If a pool is heated, covering it at night will reduce heat loss, resulting in not only warmer temperatures but an energy savings of hundreds or even thousands of dollars over the course of a year. If a pool is unheated, covering it at night can mean that in the morning, the water is comfortable rather than bone-achingly cold. Any cover, including a simple vinyl one, will help reduce heat loss. For added benefits, choose a solar cover, which contains air-filled baffles that increase the insulating value.

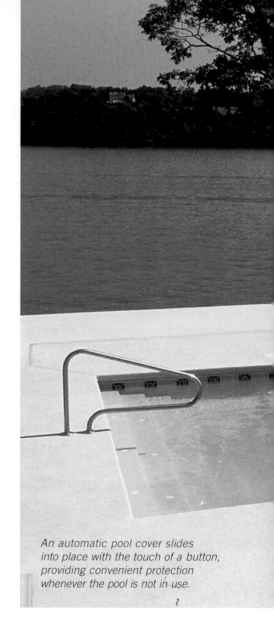

An automatic pool cover slides into place with the touch of a button, providing convenient protection whenever the pool is not in use.

A loose-fitting energy-saving cover, maneuvered into place manually, drastically reduces overnight heat loss.

COVERS FOR SAFETY

Tarps and solar covers offer no measure of safety. Anyone who steps or falls onto them would most likely end up in the water. Where safety is a primary concern, the best choice is a pool cover designed to withstand the weight of a person walking on it. Such covers, made of a tough fiberglass-mesh material, can hold loads of up to 400 pounds per square foot. Installing them manually is difficult, relegating them to use on a pool that's closed for the season. But an automatic track system makes a safety cover so easy to open and close that you can cover the pool after each use. The cover retracts out of sight when the pool is open. (See more about safety covers on page 208.)

AN AUTOMATIC OPTION

Any type of swimming pool cover can be unwieldy to maneuver into place. Because of that you may want to install an automatic system that unrolls and rolls up the cover with the turn of the key. If you're using a safety cover, an automatic system is virtually a must. Keep in mind that an automated pool cover is pricey. Installing one may cost between $8,000 and $12,000, compared to only a few hundred dollars for a simple vinyl maintenance cover.

safety tip

No matter which type of cover you use, be sure to remove it completely—rather than simply folding back a portion—before letting anyone use the pool. Swimmers can easily become trapped and disoriented if they surface beneath the cover.

pool cleaners

Even with main drains and skimmer baskets in your pool, debris is sure to accumulate, requiring additional cleaning. Hand-held skimmers are one solution, but other devices can make the job much easier. Some of them are fully automatic —eliminating cleaning from your to-do list.

VACUUMS

Aquatic vacuums connect to the intake valve in the pool's skimmer basket, working off the pool's suction and filtration system to do their cleaning. Some vacuums are manual—you maneuver them across the pool bottom much as you'd vacuum the floor of a house. Automatic vacuums motor across the pool floor on their own. For above-ground pools that contain no skimmer baskets, consider getting a self-contained "robotic" vacuum that will clean the pool automatically. Run on rechargeable batteries, these units contain their own pumps, filters, and propulsion devices and just need to be placed in the pool to do the job.

SWEEPS

A sweep connects to one of the pool's inlets and uses the pressure of rushing water to power a tail that whips around the pool, dislodging debris. Some sweeps also capture debris and store it internally, rather than sweeping debris into the main filter.

IN-FLOOR SYSTEMS

The ultimate accessory for an in-ground pool is an in-floor

A vac-sweep (above right) dislodges debris, then captures and stores it internally. A self-contained vacuum for an above-ground pool (above) uses batteries to operate its own pump and filter. An automatic pool vacuum (left) roves along the bottom of a pool, much like a vacuum inside a house.

automatic vacuum system. Such a system can cost between $3,000 and $5,000 and is installed during pool construction. Underwater jets are built into the bottom of the pool and connected to the pool's return line. When the system is switched on, the heads pop up and a booster pump creates and forces out a high-pressure swirl of water. As the water moves along the floor of the pool, it produces a strong current that forces dirt and debris toward the main drains. There, the debris is siphoned out of the pool by the main pump and transported to the filtering system.

quick tip

With any type of aquatic cleaning system, be sure to clean the basket that collects large pieces of debris. If the basket becomes clogged, the system's vacuuming capability will be seriously reduced.

pool accessories

At the top of the list of extras that can enhance your enjoyment of your swimming pool are practical accessories such as ladders and grab rails, purely recreational equipment such as slides and jump boards, and automatic controls that simplify maintenance.

Grab rails positioned by steps minimize the risk of accidents.

LADDERS AND GRAB RAILS

In addition to built-in steps that ease swimmers into the shallow end, it's smart to install ladders and grab rails in the deep end of the pool. In fact, building codes frequently require both of these aids. Ladders and easy-to-grab railings give average swimmers a place to hold onto and rest during a swim and make it easier for all pool users to get in and out of the water.

Most ladders consist of three steps, two of which extend below the water level by about 2 feet. In general, the railings on these ladders are spaced between 18 inches and 2 feet apart, which allows swimmers to fit between them comfortably as they climb in or out. Entry steps that lead into the shallow end also benefit from having a railing. If the steps are wide, a single rail installed down the center works best. Ladders and railings require careful installation by an experienced contractor, since any mistake will cause them to wobble eventually.

A fully equipped swimming pool contains everything needed for recreation as well as safety—from slides to grab rails.

As a pool safety device, horizontal rails installed just below the water line are becoming increasingly common. These grab rails provide youngsters as well as physically challenged swimmers with a ready handhold if they tire, and make the pool a safer place for all.

SLIDES

Pool slides are an increasingly popular recreational device. Though regulated and in some cases prohibited by local building codes, when properly installed they can be enjoyed without the safety concerns that often accompany diving boards.

You'll need to first make sure your pool is large enough and deep enough for a slide. An experienced contractor will be able to help you make that determination. In addition, the pool deck must be large enough to accommodate the slide. A large straight slide can measure more than a dozen feet from the ladder to the edge of the pool, but even a small slide can take up about 8 feet of deck space. Slides that curve or spiral take up less room, and can actually be more enjoyable for swimmers to use, but whichever slide design you choose, proper attachment to the deck is critical to prevent mishaps. Most builders connect

A slide can be a delightful addition to a swimming pool, and the curved shape of this one minimizes the amount of deck space used.

the slide to concrete either within or beneath the deck to ensure a sturdy base. Slides should never wobble, and should be inspected at once by a competent builder if they do.

Most slides are made from fiberglass and have a gel coating that provides an extra-slippery finish. Increasingly, pool builders are creating faux-rock slides that have a more natural look. Whatever style you decide on, be sure to have it constructed by an experienced builder.

DIVING BOARDS

Because they've fallen into disfavor with insurance companies as well as local building authorities, it is nearly impossible to add a spring-assisted diving board to most residential pools. In the few situations where they may be added, the size of the pool is the most important safety consideration. Though the exact dimensions will depend on the type of board being installed, pools should be a minimum of 8½ feet deep, 15 feet wide, and 28 feet long.

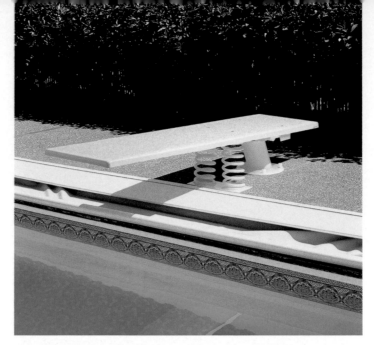

Diving boards, such as this spring-loaded one, can add thrills to a swimming pool but liability issues abound.

Diving boards are usually made of wood coated with fiberglass and covered with a nonskid surface. Maintaining the board is essential to guaranteeing safety. A warped surface or a crack in the material raises the possibility that the wood underneath has begun to rot. Replacement of the board is the only solution.

JUMP BOARDS

An alternative to adding a diving board to a new pool is to add a jump board. They are shorter and far safer than full diving boards—they're stationary rather than spring-loaded, so they don't launch a swimmer high into the air. Still, a pool must be large enough and deep enough to accommodate a jump board safely; local

Jump boards (above and left) provide a safer yet fun alternative to diving boards. Shorter and without the spring-loaded action of traditional diving boards, they lower the altitude that a diver gains—and thereby minimize the risk of mishaps.

building codes will spell out the requirements, as well as national standards (check with your pool builder for these). Unlike diving boards, most jump boards are made from aluminum—which creates a maintenance-free surface, although the nonskid coating may need occasional replacement or repair.

AUTOMATIC CONTROLS

Advances in technology have made swimming pools as easy to use—and to maintain—as turning on a TV. With the touch of a keypad, you can turn the pump on or off, adjust the heater, operate the automated cover, and switch on the lights. In addition, one touch will dispense chemicals that control water quality.

AIR SWITCHES Since water and electronic controls don't mix well, one popular design for automated controls incorporates an air switch. Air switches can be used safely at poolside because the controls don't contain any electrical connections. Instead, when a button is depressed, it sends a pulse of air through a slender hose attached to a control that triggers an electronic switch nearby.

WIRELESS CONTROLS Systems that use radio frequencies are becoming more popular. One advantage is their ability to be connected to the telephone, allowing homeowners to dial up the system while they are away so the temperature, lighting, and other features are ready when they arrive home.

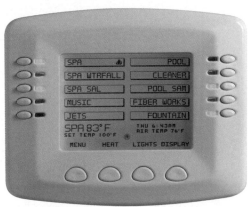

spa basics

Despite its smaller size, a spa operates in much the same way as a swimming pool. A pump circulates the water, then passes it through a filter; the addition of chemicals destroys bacteria and keeps the water sterile. There are important differences, however, between a spa and a pool. Spas are generally heated to a much higher temperature, and the force of the water flowing into the spa is much greater than that in the swimming pool—producing the high-pressure rush of water that makes spas especially soothing.

HOW A SPA WORKS

When installed next to a swimming pool, an in-ground spa uses the same equipment as the pool itself. The pool's basic equipment needs to be slightly larger to handle the additional load. Freestanding spas require their own pump, filter, and heater. That equipment can be smaller than for a swimming pool, since the workload is smaller.

Despite their ready-to-go functionality, preformed acrylic spas can easily be given a custom-made look. This slightly raised spa benefits from its stone coping.

PORTABLE SPA

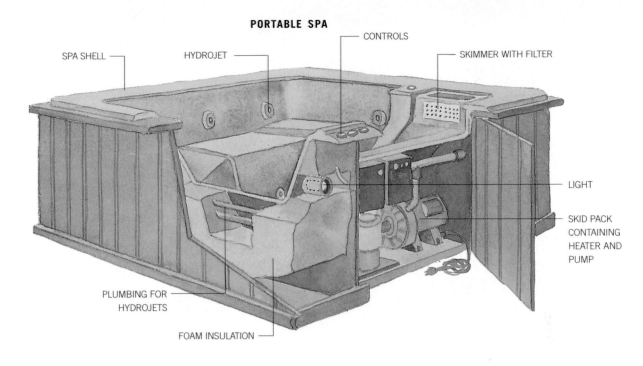

SPA SHELL

HYDROJET

CONTROLS

SKIMMER WITH FILTER

LIGHT

SKID PACK CONTAINING HEATER AND PUMP

PLUMBING FOR HYDROJETS

FOAM INSULATION

IN-GROUND SPA

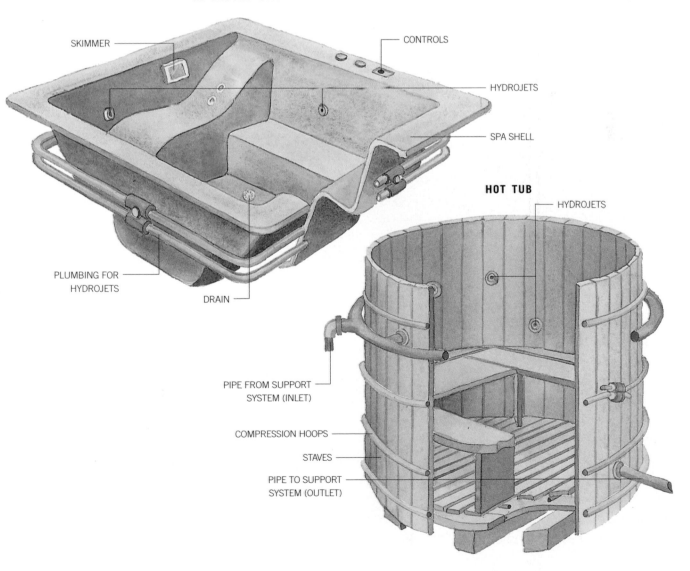

SKIMMER

CONTROLS

HYDROJETS

SPA SHELL

PLUMBING FOR HYDROJETS

DRAIN

HOT TUB

HYDROJETS

PIPE FROM SUPPORT SYSTEM (INLET)

COMPRESSION HOOPS

STAVES

PIPE TO SUPPORT SYSTEM (OUTLET)

orientation; in the best spa models, they move up and down to create a rippling massage. And in many spas, including prefabricated ones, you may be able to choose the exact location of the hydrojets. If you can, sit in the spa before you purchase it so the hydrojets can be placed according to your preference.

The air intake on a hydrojet can be regulated by opening or closing the ports near the top edge of the spa. When the ports are completely closed, hydrojets produce a gentle massage rather than a rippling one. With ports fully open, some models are able to spew out more than 75 gallons per minute, all through a single jet, to create an inviting whirlpool bath. One drawback of hydrojets is that their blowers tend to be noisy. When a spa is inside the house, this can result in

THE HYDROJETS

Hydrojets propel water into a spa, providing the high-pressure massage action so prized by spa owners. A hydrojet mixes a pressurized stream of water with air, then forces it into the spa to create a bubbling swirl. Each hydrojet pumps out between 12 and 15 gallons of water per minute, and most spas contain at least four jets. Hydrojets do not have to be fixed in one

AIR INLET

WATER INLET

FLOW RESTRICTOR

HYDROJET ACTION

unbearable sound for everyone but the spa users. But when a spa is connected to an in-ground pool, blowers can usually be located far enough from the spa, with the other pool equipment, to minimize the impact of the noise.

SPA COVERS

A cover is an essential component of a spa, not just an option. First, covers provide safety by restricting access. Second, they keep out dirt and debris, which reduces the load on the pump and filter—especially important if the spa is outdoors. Another benefit a cover provides is energy savings. Keeping the spa covered when it's not in use will greatly reduce heat loss and therefore substantially reduce your energy bills.

RIGID COVERS tend to be made of vinyl-covered foam and provide the best insulation. Buy the highest quality cover you can, because an inferior one will leak and become waterlogged. The thickness of covers varies, generally between 2 and 3 inches, and while the thinnest will suffice for indoors, the thicker models provide the best insulation for outdoor spas. Rigid covers are heavy, usually weighing 30 pounds or more, and can be difficult to maneuver.

FLEXIBLE COVERS provide a lightweight alternative. Some are filled with pockets of air that offer modest insulating value. While they offer little in the way of safety, they may suffice for your particular needs if your spa is fenced.

SPA HEATERS

While the ideal maximum temperature for a swimming pool is 78 to 82 degrees, spa water is heated much higher—in some cases, up to 104 degrees. Gas heaters are by far the fastest, warming the water in a matter of minutes. Among electric heaters, those that run on 110 volts heat water very slowly, while those that run on 220 volts are comparatively quicker. However, electric heaters are far more expensive to operate than gas heaters in most regions of the country.

SPA CONTROLS

Manual controls are ordinarily located right on the edge of the spa. They can be used to turn on the pump as well as the heater and the hydrojets, all with simple switches. Increasingly, however, spas can be adjusted from afar. Wireless controls allow adjustment from any room in the home. Telephone connections make it possible to control the settings from virtually anywhere, so you can arrive home to a spa that is heated, bubbling, and ready for use. No matter how sophisticated the controls, however, all spas have a manual override switch so you can make adjustments while you're in the spa.

A rigid cover, such as the one on this in-ground spa, provides safety and reduces heat loss.

excavating an in-ground pool

Although swimming pools conjure up thoughts of leisurely pursuits, pool construction actually begins with a bang, in the form of a major excavation project. Whether for a concrete, vinyl-lined, or fiberglass pool, this part of the process is similar to the construction of a house foundation. The following can help you chart your contractor's progress and reassure you that you're making the right choices.

The first stage of excavation for an in-ground pool involves large-scale equipment, above left. An excavator quickly digs the bulk of the hole needed.

Experienced equipment operators can navigate even complicated pool layouts with precision, above. The curved wooden forms mark the free-form perimeter.

A finished pool, right, bears no resemblance to the chaos of excavation. Good contractors make the most of a site's contours to create natural-looking settings.

PREPARING FOR EXCAVATION

Before beginning construction of an in-ground pool, a contractor will need to clear a passage at least 10 feet wide to provide sufficient access for construction equipment. This may involve cutting down trees, removing fencing, and transplanting shrubbery. The access route will also need to have a firm enough base to provide traction for the machinery. In some situations, it may be necessary to truck in gravel or other stone to support the equipment, particularly if the construction site is on a steep slope.

STAKING OUT THE SITE

After preparing the access way, the contractor will lay out the exact site of the pool for excavation. First, the perimeter of the pool is staked out, which can be done in a variety of ways—from driving wooden stakes into the ground to dusting the outline with lime. In sloping yards where a portion of the pool wall will be built aboveground and then backfilled, plywood forms will be erected. From these forms you can get a good idea of how much filling and landscaping you'll be doing after construction.

smart tip

Excavation is the most chaotic and
potentially damaging part of pool
construction. To lessen the impact
on your yard, make all decisions with
the contractor in advance, including
exactly where the access route will be,
the location for storing excavated soil,
and which specific portions of your
yard will be disturbed.

VINYL-LINED AND FIBERGLASS POOL EXCAVATION

Contractors normally begin excavation for a vinyl or fiberglass pool by using a backhoe or front-end loader to create a ramp through what will become the shallow end of the swimming pool. This allows them to move in and out of the pool with ease; when the job is finished, they will remove their equipment via the ramp.

The excavated hole will be between 6 and 12 inches bigger than the outside dimensions of the swimming pool. The additional width gives the contractor room to place the supporting walls for a vinyl-lined pool or the shell of a fiberglass pool. Once they are installed, the gap is then backfilled with sand, similar to the way a house excavation is backfilled once the concrete of the foundation walls has cured.

THE CONCRETE DIFFERENCE

In the case of a shotcrete or gunite pool, the excavation process is slightly different. Because the cuts into the earth become the forms for building the walls, they must be cut precisely in order to create the exact shape desired. If too much material is excavated, it will be difficult to build the pool as planned, because the walls can't be backfilled easily.

Rather than digging a hole larger than the pool and backfilling the gap when the walls are completed, the contractor, using heavy machinery, excavates a hole that is about 6 to 12 inches *smaller* than the pool's exterior walls. The final—and most critical—10 percent of cuts are then made by hand, with laborers using pick axes, shovels, and other hand equipment to loosen and cart away material. This hand work tends to make excavations for shotcrete or gunite pools more expensive than those for fiberglass or vinyl-lined pools.

MANAGING WET SOIL

One of the biggest problems encountered during swimming pool construction is groundwater. Any site where standing water is an issue is not a good candidate for a pool. But even where the ground appears dry, digging a hole 5 or 6 feet into the earth can sometimes yield water. This bogs down machinery and can make it difficult—though not impossible—for work to continue.

Where water is a problem, contractors will sometimes dig about 12 inches deeper into the floor of the pool than originally planned. They then add drainage piping to the floor, backfill the floor with loose gravel, and add a sump pump that connects to the drainage piping. The pump allows enough water to be drawn from the area to improve working conditions without compromising the future shape of the pool.

time-saving tip

To avoid delays caused by waterlogged soil, it's better to excavate a pool in drier months, when the water table is lower.

After a concrete in-ground pool is excavated using machinery, above, workers have to fine-tune the hole the old-fashioned way—with picks and shovels.

For a vinyl-lined pool, right, the hole is excavated entirely with heavy equipment. It is then lined with sand to create a smooth, stable surface on which the liner will rest.

building concrete pools

Concrete pools made from gunite or shotcrete require more labor and involve more details than the alternatives. In the pages that follow we describe the sequence of steps that are needed after excavation is complete.

LAYING THE FRAMEWORK

While concrete has a great deal of strength, it has little elasticity and cracks easily under stress. The most common way to address this weakness is to combine concrete with a framework of steel reinforcing rods (rebar). The result is a structure that's strong as well as resilient.

CROSS-SECTION OF A CONCRETE POOL

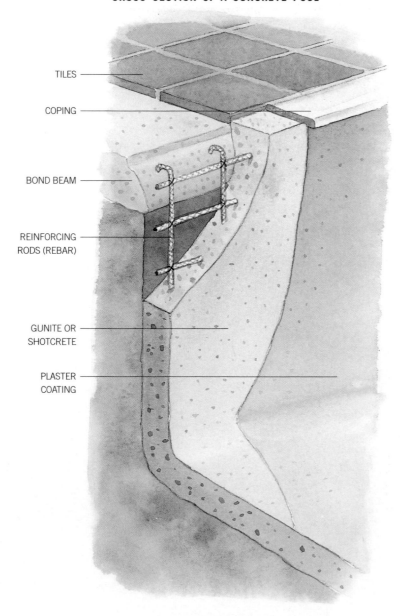

TILES

COPING

BOND BEAM

REINFORCING RODS (REBAR)

GUNITE OR SHOTCRETE

PLASTER COATING

Once excavation is complete, contractors place the rebar. The placement and amount will vary according to the project, but in general reinforcing bars are laid in an evenly spaced cross pattern to ensure uniform strength throughout. Intersecting pieces are tied together with wire to create a giant steel grid that forms the skeleton of the pool.

After the rebar is placed and tied, the plumbing system is positioned, complete with pipes connecting to the main drains and the inlets. These pipes will become embedded in the concrete when it is applied, so it is crucial for them to be positioned well— it will be nearly impossible to make changes later. To discover any plumbing leaks *before* the shotcrete or gunite is applied, a good pool contractor fills the pipes with pressurized air and monitors the pressure during construction.

The electrical wiring is also installed at this time. Rather than embedding it directly in concrete, most electricians will install a piping system known as conduit through which they thread the wiring. This way, if any repairs are needed in the future, new wiring can simply be pulled through the conduit, without the need for excavation or jackhammering.

In-ground pools built of concrete (in the form of shotcrete or gunite) allow the greatest versatility and originality in design. This elaborate pool and raised spa, left, could only be achieved using this material.

During construction of an in-ground pool, the excavated shape becomes the mold for the pool itself. Steel reinforcing rods, known as rebar, below, combine with shotcrete or grunite to give the walls resilience.

building vinyl-lined pools

Vinyl-lined pools cost significantly less than concrete pools, because of the reduced costs of the prefabricated materials as well as the simpler construction techniques. Rather than taking a month or more to complete, a vinyl-lined pool can be assembled in a matter of days following excavation.

CONSTRUCTING THE POOL WALLS

Once excavation is completed, the perimeter of the pool is filled with concrete to form footings. These are exactly analogous to footings that support concrete foundation walls in a house. When the concrete is dry, the footings are leveled and the sidewalls from the pool manufacturer are bolted together and anchored in place.

Sidewalls, made from aluminum, fiberglass, plastic, pressure-treated wood, or other materials, can be erected and sometimes braced around the perimeter of the pool in just a few hours.

With the sidewalls in place, plumbing for the main drains, skimmers, return inlets, and automatic cleaners is installed on the walls' exterior, along with any lighting or other electrical systems. The bracing that supports the sidewalls is then covered with sand or earth that was excavated from the construction site. No curing time is needed for a vinyl-lined pool.

INSTALLING THE LINER

Instead of plaster and concrete, a vinyl-lined pool incorporates a continuous piece of vinyl to create a watertight seal. To install one correctly, the floor of the swimming pool is usually covered with sand to create a smooth surface for the liner. The liner is then lowered into position, stretched taut, and fastened to the tops of the sidewalls just beneath the area where the coping will be installed. After cutting openings to accommodate the drains, skimmers, inlets, and lights, the contractor assembles the plumbing and electrical systems. As the pool is filled with water, the contractor smoothes the liner.

Once the pool walls are erected and a smooth base is prepared, the liner is set into place and attached to the tops of the walls. Since the liner arrives in one large piece, installing it is fairly quick.

CROSS-SECTION OF A VINYL-LINED POOL

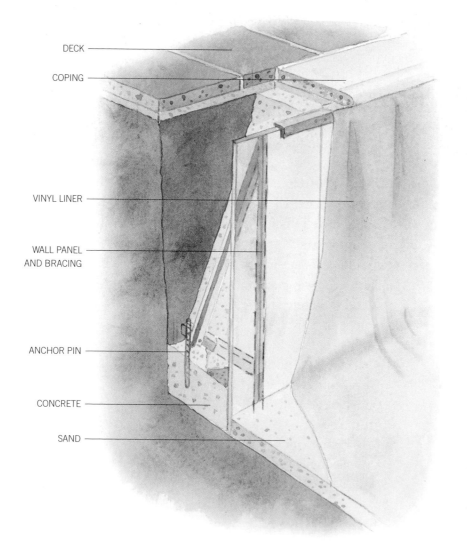

DECK

COPING

VINYL LINER

WALL PANEL AND BRACING

ANCHOR PIN

CONCRETE

SAND

Because of their ease of installation, vinyl-lined pools cost significantly less than concrete pools. When designed well, however, the overall look can be every bit as appealing.

design tip

The liners themselves are the decorative focal point of vinyl-lined pools. They come in a variety of colors and patterns, including tile motifs, that mimic the more expensive finishes of concrete pools. Be sure to consider all options carefully, since color and decoration can greatly affect the look of the finished pool.

remodeling a concrete pool

One of the advantages of shotcrete and gunite pools, compared to vinyl and fiberglass alternatives, is that they can be remodeled. You can do a simple makeover, just changing the look of your pool, or a complete coping-to-floor-drain rehab that dramatically alters the way the pool functions. Let's look at some of the methods used to remodel a pool.

THE SIMPLEST MAKEOVER

A concrete swimming pool can be reborn simply by changing the existing deck and coping material. First, the tile and top 12 inches of plaster are chiseled out, then new coping and tile are installed. When everything is set, new plaster is applied to the top portion of the wall and carefully feathered in so that the new surface and the old blend seamlessly. Depending on the type of material used for the deck and coping, this sort of project might cost between $5,000 and $8,000—well worth it, since it can vastly enhance the look of a dated swimming pool.

smart tip

Concrete swimming pools are remarkably resilient, and can be remodeled in just about all cases—even when the walls and plaster are severely cracked and don't hold water. In these cases, a fiberglass coating can be applied to create a lasting, watertight surface on top of the old one.

While stone decking takes on a formal look when the lines are straight, it creates a more natural appearance when the lines are jagged. Natural stone, which also forms the coping and lines the tops of the pool walls, can easily be added during a concrete pool makeover.

The classic design of this swimming pool, left, is accentuated by the formal lines of the decking. A feature such as this can transform any pool, whether concrete, vinyl, or fiberglass.

An existing concrete swimming pool can be radically enhanced with careful additions. Synthetic boulders, right, mimic the rustic outline of a natural coastline. These boulders can be added without changing the shape of an existing pool.

COST-BENEFIT ANALYSIS

A major swimming pool renovation is not cheap. In fact, when all the work is done, it may cost nearly as much as building an entirely new swimming pool. So why should you bother with remodeling? Because in many cases, it still makes financial sense—for one very simple reason.

In order to build a new pool, the old pool has to be demolished. This is an expensive proposition, because it includes not just the cost of labor but the extremely high cost of disposing of the heavy debris. A 16-by-32-foot rectangular pool might cost between $10,000 and $12,000 to demolish and cart away—a large amount to add to the cost of a new pool. In addition, you'll be building in what is known as disturbed or filled soil. Building on such soil requires special engineering as well as additional footings, thicker walls, and more steel rebar—all of which will require more money.

If you already have a concrete swimming pool and want to change it radically, the best thing to do is engage in a top-to-bottom renovation.

AN EXTENSIVE MAKEOVER

More extensive digging and chipping away can produce a thorough remodel of a concrete swimming pool. Such a makeover can involve digging along the sidewalls to attach plumbing systems for new returns and new drains as well as upgrading equipment such as skimmers and lighting. Walls can also be raised to deepen the pool, in combination with exterior grading. In addition, natural-rock formations, waterfalls, spillways, and integral spas can be added fairly easily.

One of the best ways to give a concrete pool a new look is to choose an alternative to a smooth plaster finish (top). One that contains small bits of marble, granite, or pebbles, such as the one above, can also provide more traction on steps.

A swimming pool newly coated with a pebbled surface will gleam when filled with water. This project might cost $10,000 to $12,000, but gives an old pool new life.

When considering a pool, homeowners tend to focus on eye-appealing details, such as the deck, landscaping, and outdoor furniture. At the center of it all, however, is the pool's principal element—water.

filling pools with water

Enjoyable as they may be, there is one inescapable downside to swimming pools: they require a great deal of water to fill: the average volume for an in-ground pool is about 20,000 gallons. Above-ground pools also need a lot of water; a pool about 15 feet in diameter can contain 5,000 gallons and a 20-by-40-foot rectangular pool can require as much as 35,000 gallons, depending on the depth. In an age of growing restrictions on water use and higher water-meter rates, the need for such large quantities of water may merit special thought.

FILLING A GUNITE OR SHOTCRETE POOL

A freshly plastered concrete pool needs to be filled immediately with water. Otherwise the plaster surface may crack and shrink and need to be recoated. But filling the pool has to be done carefully to avoid staining the walls.

A gunite or shotcrete pool lined with plaster should be filled from the bottom, usually by placing a hose at the base of the pool. When filling the pool, it is important to add the water consistently, not stopping until it reaches the tile border just beneath the coping. If a pool is filled in fits and starts, there will be pronounced high-water lines etched into the plaster walls. If water is trucked into the pool, rather than run in from a garden hose, it should be pumped in through a hose placed at the base of a wall, rather than splashed down the pool sides. Splashing it will make permanent marks on the pool walls.

Swimming pools are infrequently emptied once they've been filled

(see page 185). However, in some climates pools can lose between 1 and 2 inches of water per day, requiring daily refilling. A pool cover can drastically reduce evaporation.

FILLING A VINYL-LINED OR FIBERGLASS POOL

Pools made of these materials require less care when filling. They don't need to be filled immediately—although it's a good idea for safety's sake—and there's no risk of staining if water happens to run down the sides. Therefore, it's not necessary to place the hose in the bottom of the pool. It can simply hang over the side and be allowed to run.

AVOIDING EXCESS WATER FEES

The most convenient way to fill a swimming pool is to turn on a hose and let it flow. Depending on the rate of flow and the size of the swimming pool, filling can take between one and several days. Often, communities will charge

separate fees for water usage and for sewer use—disposing of the water. In order to avoid this double charge, which can amount to hundreds of dollars for a large swimming pool, check to see if your community allows a diversion meter to be installed in your plumbing supply system. Such a meter measures the water and waste flows separately, so that you're charged only for what goes into the pool. In many cases, the cost of installing a diversion meter is more than offset by the reduction in the disposal fee.

OPTING FOR TANKED-IN WATER

If your home is supplied by a well pump, the task of filling a swimming pool may put too much strain on your system. In this case—and in many cases where local water restrictions are in effect—it may make sense to have water brought in by a tanker truck. The fee can actually turn out to be less than the cost of water from a municipal system combined with a sewer charge. The price of trucked-in water varies, but on average costs about $35 per thousand gallons, or $350 for a 10,000-gallon pool.

money-saving tip

Water usage fees vary from municipality to municipality and can greatly affect the cost of filling a swimming pool. Check in advance with your local office about any discounts available to swimming pool owners to make sure you get the lowest possible rate.

spa construction basics

In nearly every detail, the construction of an in-ground spa, whether concrete or acrylic, mirrors that of an in-ground swimming pool. Likewise, a portable spa has much in common with an above-ground swimming pool, especially in preparing the site before positioning the pool.

The simplest way to build a spa is to add one during construction of an in-ground pool. This lessens the construction costs compared to building one separately, and ensures that construction will proceed smoothly, without damaging the main pool.

CONCRETE SPAS

Right down to the smallest feature, a shotcrete or gunite spa is built the same way as an in-ground pool made of the same material. As with a pool, about 90 percent of the hole for the spa has to be machine-excavated, with the remaining 10 percent dug by hand. When that is done, a grid built of steel reinforcing rod is assembled to form the spa skeleton. The rebar is also used to create any steps or benches the spa will contain. When this work is completed, the plumbing, including the drains and inlets for the hydrojets, and the electrical wiring are attached.

Next, the gunite or shotcrete is applied under pressure, sprayed directly against the rebar so that all pockets of air are eliminated. When the spraying is completed, the material is troweled smooth and allowed to cure for several weeks. The next step is either tiling or applying a layer of plaster to form the surface coating. As with swimming pools, coping material is usually placed along the top of the spa, to create a transition to the deck and surrounding landscape.

A spa complements an in-ground pool in every way. Its warmer temperature provides a welcome haven from the cooler waters of the pool, and its scale creates an intimate zone for relaxation.

IN-GROUND ACRYLIC AND FIBERGLASS SPAS

Installing an in-ground acrylic or fiberglass spa is nearly identical to installing a fiberglass swimming pool, although far less effort is needed because of the spa's significantly smaller size. Get the guidance of a contractor or an engineer to determine the right spot to site the spa. The excavated hole will be slightly larger than the spa in all directions. When the excavation is complete, the hole is lined with sand that is molded to conform to the shape of the spa. It is essential that no pockets of air exist when the spa is set in place, to keep the spa shell from caving in and ultimately developing leaks. Once the spa is in place, the electrical and plumbing systems can be installed. Then the gap between the hole and the spa should be backfilled with sand to provide firm support.

ADDING A SPA TO AN EXISTING POOL

When adding a spa to an existing swimming pool—whether concrete, vinyl-lined, or fiberglass—there are several factors to consider. First, the spa cannot be built directly adjacent to the pool, nor can the wall of the existing pool be cut into to any significant degree. If either of these is done, the pool's structure can become compromised and may even collapse. Instead, the spa needs to be built away from the pool wall by at least 2 feet. An engineer or experienced contractor should determine the exact location. However, the spa can still be connected to the pool via a spillway or waterfall, providing an integrated appearance without weakening the pool's structure. In most cases, the spa can be connected to the pool's plumbing and electrical systems fairly easily, though this is also a job for an experienced contractor.

An in-ground spa, such as this idyllic terraced one, can easily be added to an existing pool—provided construction does not weaken the pool's structure. A contractor can best determine how close it can safely be located.

Portable outdoor spas offer easy-to-position mobility. Because of their weight when filled, they require firm support from underneath, often in the form of a concrete, gravel, or sand base (left).

Since portable spas are almost always tended to by homeowners rather than professionals, the mechanical equipment should be configured for easy access. A hatch, shown below, makes maintenance a breeze.

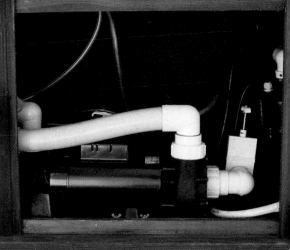

INSTALLING A PORTABLE SPA

Portable spas are easy to set up, but require special care to guarantee long life and to ensure that the manufacturer's warranty remains in effect. For outdoor installation, the spa will need to be placed on either a concrete platform (see page 40) or a 6-to-12-inch bed of sand on carefully leveled soil.

If a spa is positioned on a deck or porch, its tremendous weight may have to be supported by a system of posts and piers. Be sure to consult a contractor or an engineer to make certain the spa poses no danger. Portable spas can also be installed indoors, in which case it's essential to choose an appropriate location (see page 41).

FILLING A SPA

Spas are easily filled with a garden hose. They lose slightly less water to evaporation than swimming pools because of their smaller surface area, but they may need water added two to three times a week to remain full. Putting on a cover can dramatically reduce evaporation.

planning your landscape

Every successful landscape design begins with a single question: What do I want from this space? Although the specific answers vary from one homeowner to the next, there are several broad goals that apply to the setting for any pool or spa. Start your planning process by considering these basic aims and by deciding where each one falls on your list of priorities. The knowledge will be crucial when you move ahead with your project, especially if you choose to do the work in phases.

AESTHETICS

It's true that beauty is in the eye of the beholder, and it's also true that beauty is far more important to some people than to others. For instance, to some pool owners, all that really matters is a good swim (spa owners may just want a nice long soak in a hot tub). These people are not much concerned

With its stone edging and dark interior, this spa gives the illusion of a natural pond. Native plantings; a tiny, trickling stream; and a setting at the far edge of the yard add to the feeling of rural seclusion.

For the owners of this pool, outdoor living was a top priority when it came time for landscaping. The result: a poolscape with all the comforts of home, including a covered kitchen and space for family dining.

convenient to the pool or spa these facilities are, the more pleasure they'll bring—and the more they'll discourage the flow of traffic through your house.

When space is tight, your sanity-savers will be landscape elements that do multiple jobs—for instance, benches that also store furniture, sports gear, or garden tools; or a fire pit whose cover converts it to a low table or extra seating. Easy access to your pool from more than one part of your house will provide flexibility, but may require an alarm or self-locking doors if small children are on the scene.

with how well the particular body of water suits its setting. At the other extreme are people who rarely take a dip. Their pleasure comes from the sight of an elegant pool blended seamlessly with its surroundings. Chances are you fall somewhere between those two opposites. But where? Your answer will determine not only the details of your landscaping plan but also how long you're willing to wait for it to be completed.

CONVENIENCE AND FLEXIBILITY

Consider all the pool-related activities on your agenda, such as cooking and eating, entertaining, showering, and changing. Also consider how many people might be involved in these functions. Then incorporate into your plan all the areas or structures required to handle your needs. The more

all in good time
■ ■ ■

No law says you have to install your entire landscape in one fell swoop—especially if you're undecided about such factors as the kind of paving you want for your pool deck or whether to use a wall, fence, or hedges to gain privacy. Why rush into something you may regret, or even wind up tearing out a few years down the road? Here are some ideas for temporary solutions to long-term goals.

- Have your pool installed in your lawn with just a broad coping (see page 117) and leave the decking for later. Just be careful when you mow, so that grass clippings don't end up in the water.
- Erect whatever safety fencing the law and your peace of mind require, but improvise on privacy screens. For example, inexpensive wire mesh covered with annual vines; stands of tall, bushy, fast-growing annuals; or freestanding screens, with or without plants, will all provide seclusion while you debate the merits of other, more permanent options.
- Let a pavilion or other large shade structure wait until next year—or even the year after. In the meantime, shield loungers from the sun with patio umbrellas or colorful canvas panels attached to tall stakes.
- Rather than build a pool-side changing room now, pitch a tent. You can either buy a tent and keep it in place all season long, or rent one from a catering-supply house at pool-party time.

A solid masonry wall provides the ultimate in safety, privacy, and ease of maintenance. The one above, made of cream-colored poured concrete, also offers a stunning counterpoint to its rugged mountain backdrop.

The owners of this home (right) considered both climate and aesthetics when they chose their pool's decking. Textured concrete, bordered by mellow brick, sails through the rigors of a northern winter and blends beautifully with the formal landscape beyond.

SAFETY

Safety is the top priority in any pool landscaping scheme. Many communities mandate security fencing as well as self-closing, self-latching, self-locking gates. (Even where these features are not required by law, your mind will rest easier with them in place.) Passageways near the pool need to be well defined and unobstructed, with firm traction and good lighting. (See more about safety on pages 200 to 209.)

PRIVACY AND COMFORT

As is the case with aesthetics, people vary quite a bit in their thoughts about privacy. If it ranks near the top of your priority list, include fences, walls, dense trees, or hedges in your plan, to block the view of your pool or spa from anyplace outside your yard. Depending on your climate, you may also want to add structures or plantings that block intense sun and wind—or you may need to remove shade-casting obstacles in order to provide more warmth.

EASE OF MAINTENANCE

With maintenance costs on the rise, and your own time at a premium, you'll want to choose your landscaping palette carefully. Easy-care winners include masonry surfaces that need no painting, rustproof and water-resistant furniture, and plants that thrive naturally in your climate while dropping a minimum of leaves, flowers, and fruit.

This pool and spa combo is a low-maintenance winner, thanks to an easy-care planting scheme, rugged stone walls, and tough but comfortable furniture.

working with a professional
■ ■ ■

There is much satisfaction to be had in pointing to a stunning pool-side landscape and saying, "I did it all myself." The fact is, though, that even if you have the time, skill, and energy to do the job from start to finish, there are good reasons to enlist the help of professionals, especially during the design phase. Not the least of these reasons is that, while you may not be on top of all the breaking news, good landscape architects and designers have up-to-the-minute knowledge of changing building codes, safety regulations, materials, and technologies. Their savvy advice may lead you to creative options you didn't know existed— or save you from costly mistakes. But to get the most from your relationship with a pro, it pays to do a little homework first.

■ Find your style. Peruse photographs in magazines and books. Go on local garden tours that include homes with pools. In each case, note which shapes, colors, plants, and materials appeal to you and why. Take photographs and clip articles. The more you can tell—and show—your future design helper about your likes, dislikes, and expectations, the more likely you'll be happy with the final result.

■ Find your comfort range. Consider the complexity of your project, your level of experience, and the size of your budget—then decide how much you want to tackle. You may opt simply to get some basic design advice, then grab the ball and run with it. Or you may do the plant-related tasks yourself but rely on subcontractors for wiring, paving, and construction work. Or you may let pros do the job from start to finish.

■ Find the right match. When it comes to a project as subjective as your own backyard, don't settle for the first name that leaps out from the Yellow Pages. When you're on a garden tour and find an appealing poolscape, ask who designed it. Solicit referrals from friends and neighbors. Other good sources of leads include nearby universities with landscape-architecture programs and the staffs of upscale nurseries and garden-accessory shops.

YOUR LANDSCAPE'S INFRASTRUCTURE

Once you've defined the broad goals for your landscape, take a good look at the elements within it. In one sense, your choices are governed only by your taste and budget, but in each case there are some practical guidelines to keep in mind.

On a hillside so steep that many people would shrug their shoulders and walk away, the owners of the spa above have created a haven for outdoor living. The simple secret: a series of interconnected, stepped-down decks. The fence, with its wagon-wheel pattern, both unifies the scene and creates a barrier that prevents small children and pets from toppling to the ground far below.

Eager swimmers often take the shortest route to the pool—even if that means cutting through a flowerbed. The simplest way to avoid trampled plants: install a steppingstone path (right).

cost-saving tip

If you know you want to add a water feature at some point but you're not sure exactly what kind—or if it's just not in the budget right now—at least have your pool contractor install any additional plumbing lines that you're likely to need. That way, you'll avoid the trouble and expense of adding them later.

WIRING Nothing adds more to the allure of a pool or spa than good lighting. Fountains and other water features also demand wiring for electric pumps. Most likely some of your pool-related tasks will require the help of a pro, but it's easy to install low-voltage lighting yourself (see page 173).

IRRIGATION Depending on your plant choices and your climate, you may want to install a permanent irrigation system, either drip or sprinkler style, to make watering easier and more efficient. At the very least, make sure you have hose hookups in convenient locations.

DECKING The surface around your pool or spa can range from a paved strip that's just wide enough for easy walking to a series of interconnected patios and terraces made with anything from concrete pavers to handcrafted tile (see pages 144 to 146).

STAIRS AND PATHWAYS Spend some time pondering how you and your guests will move from house to pool to the broader landscape. Your options for surfacing paths and steps are even wider than they are for patios and decks, but some basic guidelines do apply (see page 147).

WATER FEATURES Of course you can enjoy your daily dip without a water slide, waterfall, or fountain, but these and other water features can add drama, elegance, or just plain fun to your landscape. Although installation is best done while your pool is being built, it is possible to add many of these structures later. To add a fountain that connects to your pool's return lines, you'll need the help of a professional pool technician (see page 169 for one such project).

putting your plan on paper
■ ■ ■

Even if you intend to hire a professional landscape architect or designer, it's a good idea to get your own ideas down on paper first. That task will be simpler if you use overlays, as described on page 46. This technique is especially helpful if you plan to complete your landscaping in phases, but it's also a great way to try out a variety of hardscape and planting schemes without having to redraw your entire plan each time. If you already have a plot plan that shows your pool or spa in place, that's your starting point. Otherwise, you'll need a large sheet of graph paper (ideally at least 16 by 20 inches) and sheets of tracing paper of the same size.

On the graph paper, draw your master plan—that is, your yard as it will be (or already is) with the pool or spa in place. Include your house and all plantings, hardscape, or structures that you regard as permanent. Also note the direction of prevailing winds, sources of unwanted noise, as well as views that you want to either block or emphasize—for instance, a vista of sea, mountains, or city lights. Leave out anything that's currently in your yard but that you plan to eliminate, such as trees that would shade the pool or lights that cast too much glare. Be sure to indicate north on your plan so you'll know the path the sun will follow across the site.

To save space and avoid confusion, use symbols or colors to denote plants and other design elements, and make a master key that explains what each symbol means.

Tape a sheet of tracing paper over your master plan and sketch the additions you intend to make, such as a pathway and plantings. If you'll be completing your project over time, use a separate sheet for each phase of the work. To use this technique as a brainstorming method, simply make a different overlay for each set of variations you come up with. Ultimately, you may wind up cutting and pasting together pieces from several of your sketches to reach your dream scheme.

surrounding surfaces

Strictly speaking, you don't need to have decking around your pool—a simple coping that caps its walls and joins it to the surrounding lawn works just fine. But smooth, flat, stable surfaces provide an added dimension to pool-side life, giving you attractive, comfortable spaces for dining, entertaining, playing games, or just hanging out.

POOL DECKING

When it comes to pool decking, you have a multitude of materials to choose from. But the good ones all have several things in common.

FIRM, COMFORTABLE FOOTING It's important to remember that people who tread this surface will do so with bare, wet feet. Look for materials that reflect rather than

Stone decking (left) is a perfect choice to complement the clean-lined modern architecture of this house. Brick (below left) has a warm look and can be laid in a variety of patterns. Choose brick that has some texture to avoid a slippery surface. Wood (below right) sets a casual tone. Unfortunately, it's prone to splintering; often slippery when wet; and vulnerable to damage by insects, water, and sunlight.

A lush, green lawn is restful to the eye and more welcoming to bare feet than any hard-surface decking material. Here, a wide coping of flagstone matches the landscape's other paved surfaces.

absorb heat and that provide good traction without being coarse, uneven, or prone to splintering.

EASE OF MAINTENANCE Choose a surface that's easy to sweep or hose down—it will be the barrier between the pool and the rest of your landscape and will catch leaves, grass clippings, and all manner of other debris. Regardless of what it's made of, make sure the deck slopes away from the pool's coping by ¼ to ⅜ inch per foot. This will allow hose or rain water to drain away freely, and will prevent water splashed out of the pool from flowing back in.

STAYING POWER Even more than most other outdoor surfaces, a pool deck takes a beating. Choose a material that will resist algae, bacteria, chemicals, frost, and fungi—not to mention your pets' occasional indiscretions—as well as hard knocks from toppled furniture or mishandled lawn tools.

GOOD LOOKS It goes without saying that you want your deck to be attractive, but also keep in mind how it will blend with its surroundings. Seek out materials that complement the colors and textures of other paved areas as well as the architecture of your house.

Composite decking offers the appearance, solid feel, and easy workability of wood with none of its drawbacks. Made from a combination of reclaimed wood and recycled plastic, it never splinters and provides excellent traction even when wet. And, unlike wood, it resists moisture, insects, and sunlight—so the only maintenance required is an occasional hosing-down.

This pool's time had come for a total makeover. The first step: scrapping the fence, now that the children of the house are grown. When removing the deteriorating deck proved too time-consuming, the owners simply topped it with flagstone. The painted-brick wall was resurfaced with tile and adorned with twin lion-head fountains. (For more of this Cinderella story, see page 169.)

The naturally irregular shapes of the deck's flagstones seem pleasingly random. In fact, though, many were carefully cut and pieced together around the pool.

Once in place, stair treads were rounded to ensure comfortable walking. Then the whole deck was hosed down to remove dust and debris.

In the final step, a mason applies custom-tinted grout with a bag that resembles a giant pastry tube.

smart tip

smart tip

Reserve gravel, wood chips, and similar particles for paths, sitting areas, and planting beds that are far removed from the pool. Such small chunks migrate with amazing ease, and can make pool maintenance a nightmare.

Gently rising concrete stairs, above, echo the color and angle of the rugged "hillside" behind this spa.

The soft gray tones of pea gravel, right, provide a foil for colorful flowers. On the garden paths, the gravel is loose; at poolside, it's safely embedded in concrete.

STAIRS, PATHWAYS, AND PATIOS

The farther an area is from the water's edge, the more options you have in surface materials. Firm footing is still crucial, but skin-pleasing textures and temperatures are not. Therefore, you can freely use darker paving that might become too hot for bare feet, or wood decking that could deliver painful splinters. As with your pool deck, though, you will still want to consider texture and color, ease of maintenance, weather resistance, and drainage capability.

fences and walls

A good fence or wall can be the hardest-working element in your landscape. Of course, equipped with a secure gate it helps ensure your privacy and peace of mind. Chosen with care and strategically placed, however, a fence or wall can do much more than that. It can also conceal pool gear; screen unwanted views; shield you from harsh sun, chilly winds, or glaring lights; muffle noise; carve a broad, bland expanse into welcoming "rooms"; provide vertical planting space—and shine as an object of beauty in its own right.

In heavily populated areas, municipalities generally enforce strict fencing guidelines. But sometimes, in an isolated setting like this one, with no small children on the scene, pool owners are bound only by their own taste and imagination. Here, a wooden picket fence partially surrounds a pool that could almost pass for an old swimming hole. On the far side, nothing blocks the vista of densely wooded hills.

A solid, locked gate (above left), flanked by stone pillars and slatted fencing, will prevent even the most determined tyke from breaking and entering. High stone walls (above right) form a veritable fortress, guarding this raised lap pool from small, unwanted visitors.

PLAYING IT SAFE

Many towns and cities have regulations that specify the height of a fence surrounding a pool, the maximum size of any gaps within it, and whether or not the gate must have a self-closing mechanism. Laws regarding the extent of a fence also vary. Some communities require pools to be fenced on all four sides while others need just the yard to be fenced—the house counts as the fourth side provided certain safety devices are installed on it. Before you begin the design process, check with your local authorities about relevant ordinances. Confer with your insurance agent, too: your liability policy may mandate precautions over and above those required by the building code. For more on pool and spa safety, including basic fencing guidelines, see pages 200 to 209.

reducing wind
■ ■ ■

When wind is a problem, the style of your fence can make a big difference. For example, wind rushes over a solid fence like a stream of water. Such a barrier provides little or no wind protection past the distance equal to its height (figure 1). To reduce wind flow, use fencing with openings at least ½ inch but no more than 4 inches wide.

Another possibility is to add a baffle to a solid fence to increase its wind-blocking ability:

To extend wind protection to a distance of approximately twice the height of the fence, angle a baffle 45 degrees into the wind (figure 2).

Eliminate the downward rush of wind by using a baffle angled 45 degrees with the wind. You'll feel warmest in the pocket below the baffle and at a distance equal to a little more than the fence height (figure 3).

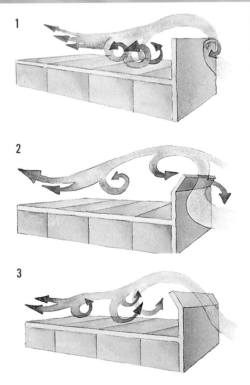

CHOOSING A FENCE

You'll want a fence or wall that complements both your house and the other features in your landscape. However, that needn't limit your choice of materials or break your budget. Wood, iron, and aluminum can all form fences that range from rustic to grand. Even chain link and wire mesh can be disguised with vines, thick shrubs, or inexpensive facing panels. For fences that are close

A high board fence with narrow openings ensures safety and privacy while admitting soft breezes and filtered sunlight. It's also a perfect match for this woodsy setting.

to the pool, use the most moisture-resistant materials you can find. Good choices include redwood or cedar heartwood, which naturally resist water; lumber made from recycled plastic; and rust-resistant, noncorrosive metals.

POOL SCREENS

When security is not a factor, an attractive screen can perform all the space-defining, environment-altering feats of a fence, often at a fraction of the cost. You might choose panels made from bamboo, reed, canvas, wood, safety glass, or translucent plastic; or plant a living screen of shrubs or trees. Either way, the result can be simple or elaborate, portable or stationary.

A handful of interconnected, freestanding screens provide all the enclosure this spa needs. Besides shielding soakers from passing traffic, the panels support climbing vines, while the broad, slatted top casts welcome shade at midday.

building a freestanding screen

This quick and easy privacy screen is composed of two lath grids in simple frames that are joined with hinges, but you can devise numerous variations on the theme. For instance, you can add more grids, sink the uprights into sand for portability, or fasten the grids to the back of a raised planting bed. Choose naturally decay-resistant wood, such as redwood or cedar heartwood, or, better yet, a lumber composite made from recycled plastic.

Build the lath grid before sizing the frame. Join the finished frames with three bifold hinges. To sink the posts in sand, dig three 2-foot-deep holes (the center hole needs to be wide enough to accommodate two 2 by 4s), pour 4 inches of sand in the bottom of each hole, and position the posts. Then fill the holes with more sand, packing it in firmly.

1 Lay the lath uprights face down on a flat surface, then lay out the crosspieces. Space the pieces equidistantly, on approximately 8-inch centers, to make the grid. Place a dab of waterproof glue where the pieces cross. Then nail or screw each intersection. When the finished grid is flipped over, the fasteners will be out of sight.

2 Size the frame pieces to fit around the finished grid, with the sides of the frame flanking the top piece. Use waterproof glue and countersunk screws to join the sides to the top.

3 Slide the lath grid inside the frame. Drive in screws from the sides of the frame to keep the grid in place.

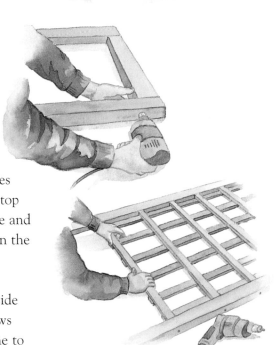

MATERIALS LIST
- Waterproof glue
- Nails or screws
- Three bifold hinges

For each grid:
- Six 1-by-2 uprights 5 feet long
- Nine 1-by-2 crosspieces 3½ feet long

For each frame:
- Two 2-by-4 posts 7½ feet long
- One 2-by-4 crosspiece 3½ feet long

plants around your pool

A central part of a successful landscape design is careful plant selection. Plants should suit your taste, complement your house and its surroundings, and thrive in the available growing conditions. When your landscape happens to contain a swimming pool or spa, plant selection demands some additional considerations.

A POOL'S MICROCLIMATE

The area around a swimming pool is a harsh environment for plants. Chlorinated water and pool chemicals may be splashed on them, sometimes with fatal results. Strong sunlight, intensified by water and pavement, can burn delicate flowers and foliage. The pool itself, especially if it's heated, will raise the humidity in the immediate area, promoting mildew in susceptible plants. Finally, the first foot or so of ground next to a paved area—be it flowerbed or lawn—will probably receive more than its fair share of water from splashes and hosing off the deck. If all this makes you want to paint trompe l'oeil flowers everywhere, take heart: plenty of beautiful plants are rugged enough to take just about everything your pool's microclimate can dish out.

To make wise choices, take notice of which plants grow well for your pool-owning neighbors. Chances are they'll perform like troupers in your yard, too. Gardening guides written for your area can also give you good insight into which plants will thrive.

A high-desert setting (above), with its dry soil and harsh sun, can be hard on plants—and the people who must maintain them. The owners of this pool have chosen wisely, relying on native plants and Mediterranean herbs that thrive naturally in hot, dry conditions.

In an open landscape, the spa at left, with its edging of rugged boulders, could look contrived. But surrounded by trees and shade-loving shrubs, it's almost a dead ringer for a natural hot spring.

The plants at water's edge soften the jagged rocks, but are tough enough to handle both reflected heat and the chemical-laced splashes from the pool.

planting tip

Plants that are classified as full-sun lovers may need some shade if they're subjected to the reflected light of a swimming pool.

153

PUTTING PLANTS TO WORK

No matter which part of your pool's surroundings you want to alter or improve, how and where you place your plants will make all the difference.

THE VIEW Hedges and trellised vines are classic choices for blocking an unpleasant view. But even strategically placed window boxes can shield you from a sight you'd rather leave unseen. When you've got the opposite challenge—a dramatic vista that you want to emphasize—a bold specimen plant or two can play the scene for all it's worth.

WIDE-OPEN SPACES Whatever is on the agenda—from entertaining a crowd to curling up with a good book—plants can help you carve one large (or not-so-large) area into separate "rooms."

NOISE A dense hedge will help muffle sounds, but to really fight noise pollution combine thick plantings with walls, fences, and fountains. (For more on water features, see pages 168 to 169.)

BRIGHTENING THE SCENE In a dim woodland setting, or for nighttime entertaining, call on plants with white foliage and flowers. They'll sparkle among the trees and after dusk in a way that even pastel blooms can't match.

Two palm trees, standing like sentinels, direct the eye across the flat foreground toward the distant mountains.

With ceramic-tile walls and decking and a sleek curtain of falling water, this pool area (above left) could appear somewhat harsh and uninviting. But carefully chosen succulents and herbs, spilling over their small bed, soften the sharp edges and flat surfaces. Burgundy foliage echoes the subtle, varied red tones of the tiles.

Gently flowing curves set an easy tone in this sleek—almost minimalist—landscape (above right). Waves of ceramic tile on the pool's bottom are echoed in the decking, stairs, and patio. The theme continues in the lawn, which was planted in alternating ripples of fescue and bluegrass.

time-saving tip

A swimming pool looks lovely surrounded by a lush, green lawn. But if that's the setting you choose, mow with care (or supervise your mowing crew) so that grass clippings don't wind up in the water.

HEDGE YOUR BETS

Whether you use them alone or in combination with walls and fences, hedges can perform a variety of tasks in your landscape, from guarding privacy to providing a dramatic backdrop for colorful flowers. Here are some tips to help you get the most from your green screen.

THINK AHEAD Purchase trees or shrubs that will be the size you need when they reach maturity. Don't be tempted by nursery stock that's "just perfect" now. In just a few years, those plants could grow into monsters that block your sun and take over your garden.

The owners of the tiny pool above found an excellent way to gain privacy without sacrificing space. The trunks of the pear trees hug the fence while their bushy canopies block the water from view.

Rows of graceful palm trees (facing page) partially screen this lap pool from the rest of the yard while their fronds lightly shade its surface. It is a pretty scene, but planting trees this close to a pool is risky: Their roots could crack the sides.

CONSULT TOWN HALL BEFORE YOU PLANT Many communities have guidelines designed to protect solar access or beautiful views.

BEWARE OF SPEED DEMONS Before you zero in on fast-growing plants, consider two things. First, if you want to maintain a formal or semi-formal style, rapid growers will demand almost constant clipping. Second, the trees and shrubs that grow quickly generally have shorter

life spans than those with more moderate growth rates. If you're eager to achieve a lush, mature look right away, fill in with perennials for a few years.

THINK OUT AS WELL AS UP If your yard is small, a hedge might provide privacy but eat up half the available space. Maybe what you need isn't a hedge at all, but a vine-covered trellis or a few trees espaliered against a wall or fence.

plants to keep at a distance

How well your plants will grow is only one factor in their suitability for a pool-side landscape. Their growth habits are also important—and become more so the closer they are to the water's edge. Here are some things to think about as you peruse catalogs or stroll down nursery aisles.

PROBLEM	SOME PRIME CULPRITS
PLANT LITTER To avoid plant debris in the water, situate plants that drop leaves or flowers away from the pool. Likewise, keep plants that drop fruit or sap away from the pool deck as well as the water. Otherwise, you'll be asking for permanent stains, a slippery surface, and a lot of stinging insects flying in for sweet treats.	bougainvillea fruit trees and bushes (all) New Guinea impatiens willow *(Salix)* wisteria
INVASIVE ROOTS Trees, shrubs, and rampant perennials that spread their roots far and wide can buckle your pavement and clog your water pipes. At best they'll make high-maintenance nuisances of themselves.	bamboo California fuchsia poplar *(Populus)* silver grass *(Miscanthus)* willow *(Salix)*
MILDEW All the humidity around a pool can encourage mildew. Steer clear of plants that are prone to the disease.	asters bee balm *(Monarda)* black-eyed Susan *(Rudbeckia)* garden phlox *(Phlox paniculata)* roses *(Rosa)*
BEE ATTRACTANTS Yes, they add beauty and fragrance to your landscape. But they also attract bees, which you probably don't want joining the fun, so don't plant them right at the water's edge.	bee balm *(Monarda)* bottlebrush *(Callistemon)* borage buttonbush *(Cephalanthus occidentalis)* cosmos *(Cosmos bipinnatus)* honeysuckle *(Lonicera)* star jasmine *(Trachelospermum)*
PRICKLY OR IRRITATING PLANTS Keep these far from the pool edge, so people don't brush against them with bare legs.	barberry *(Berberis)* cacti pyracantha roses *(Rosa)* rue *(Ruta graveolens)*

GO FOR THE GREEN

You may want to eschew both decking and pool-side planting beds in favor of a lush, green lawn. Few sights are lovelier or more relaxing than the cool interplay of blue water against green grass. And few surfaces are more welcoming to bare feet and wet bodies than a carpet of turf. If that's the setting you choose, keep these guidelines in mind.

LEAVE A BROAD BUFFER Installing an extra-wide coping around your pool will make mowing easier and help ensure that grass clippings don't wind up in the water.

BE PREPARED TO COMPROMISE The grasses that form the softest, most toe-tickling lawns perform best in cool weather, and they demand a lot of water. If your climate can't meet those standards, chances are you can still achieve your blanket of green by planting warm-season grasses or low-growing ground covers. But don't expect the same cushiony feeling you'd get from, say, Kentucky bluegrass.

BROADEN YOUR HORIZONS Instead of turf grass or as an accent to your lawn, consider planting ornamental grasses. They require little maintenance, they thrive in the harsh light and reflected heat from paved surfaces, and most varieties deposit little litter. In addition their soft, billowy textures provide a perfect complement to the flat smoothness of water—or close-clipped turf.

espaliering

Training a tree or other plant to grow more or less flat against a wall or fence is a classic trick for saving space as well as a great way to keep flowering or fruiting branches a safe distance from the water's edge.

MATERIALS LIST

- Trellis or wire
- Pruning shears
- Soft cloth or plastic ties

1 At planting time, choose two strong branches to form the tree's first tier; remove all other shoots and cut back the leader (the main trunk) to just above the bottom wire. Bend the branches at a 45-degree angle and secure them to the wire with soft cloth or plastic ties (not wire).

2 During the first growing season, continually and gradually tighten the ties so that by season's end the branches are horizontal. When the newly sprouted leader is long enough, hold it so it's erect and tie it to the second wire.

3 During the first dormant season, cut back the leader close to the second wire. Choose two branches for the second tier and prune off all competing shoots. Cut the lateral growth on the first-tier branches back to three buds.

4 During the second growing season, gradually bring the second-tier branches to a horizontal position, as described in Step 2. Keep the leader upright and tie it to the third wire.

5 Repeat the process for a fourth wire if you have one. When the leader reaches the top wire, cut it back to just above the top branch. Keep horizontal branches in bounds by pruning back the ends to downward-facing side branches in the late spring and summer.

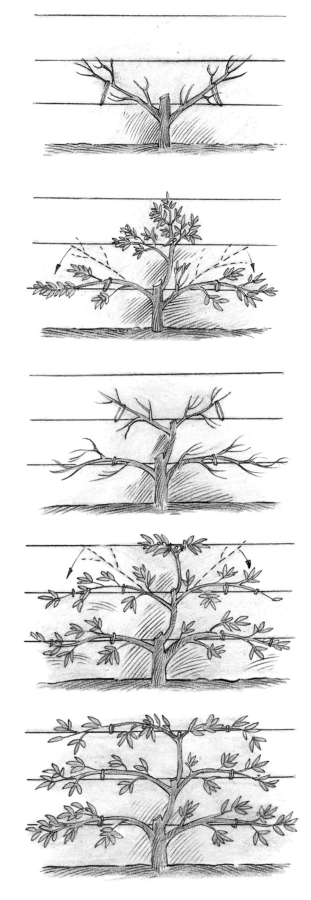

paradise in pots

If your pool or spa and the surrounding pavement consume most of the space in your small yard, a container garden may be your only planting option. But even with acres of land at your disposal, you have plenty of good reasons to grow some plants in pots.

ARCHITECTURE ON THE GO

Because potted plants are portable, they make all-but-instant space dividers. You can gather them into an island bed, line them up to form a privacy hedge, or push them back against a wall when you need an open "party room."

A BROADER PALETTE

Containers let you indulge your taste for plants that wouldn't grow well—and might not even survive—in your setting. For instance, you can amend potting mix to suit any plant's requirements for texture, nutrients, or pH level. (In the ground, such soil-boosting measures will take you only so far.) You can whisk potted shade lovers to shelter when the sun gets too harsh, or move sun worshippers out of the shadows and into the light as necessary. Delicate specimens such as citrus trees, bougainvillea, passionflowers, and a multitude of tender herbs can sail through the summer on a northern patio, then spend the winter ensconced in a greenhouse or sunny window.

In a paved courtyard, a few trees in narrow beds are the only in-ground greenery. But massed container plants surround the pool with a lush garden.

INSTANT GRATIFICATION

Watching your gardening efforts unfold each year at nature's pace can be both inspiring and gratifying. But there is also much to be said for buying pots of flowers in full bloom and setting them around the deck of your pool. With plants in containers, you also get to orchestrate the show from start to finish. For instance, when your spring tulips and daffodils pass their prime, you just move them out of the way and carry in replacements.

Potted plants (right), clustered at the ends of this pool, add softness and color while leaving plenty of room for swimmers to move around on the decking.

Because container plants are so portable, you can place them right at the water's edge for a decorative effect (for instance, at pool-party time), then move them out of the way when swimmers need room to enter and exit.

the great indoors

■ ■ ■

In recent years, the popularity of indoor pools and spas has grown by leaps and bounds, especially in northern climates, and the trend shows no sign of stopping. It's no wonder. Who wants to go to the trouble and expense of installing a pool that can be used only for a few months of the year? As practical as it may be, though, an indoor pool comes equipped with a challenge: how to avoid the look and feel of a health club or chain hotel setting. The answer: container plants. They can help make your indoor space look like an outdoor paradise or a living room that just happens to contain a small body of water—the choice is yours. (Savvy furniture choices help, too. For more on that, see page 174.)

pool-side structures

In one way, swimming pools and spas are like babies: in relation to their size, they seem to require an enormous amount of equipment, and new pool owners—like new parents—must find someplace to put it all. The obvious solution is a pool-side building designed for the purpose.

There are plenty of other reasons for adding structures near your pool. For instance, you may want a covered space for entertaining, lounging, or even working on your laptop computer. Or perhaps you just want to protect your home's interior from all those wet towels and bathing suits. Whatever the size of your property or your budget, options abound for both specialized and multipurpose structures. If installing your pool or spa puts a dent in your resources, erect the minimum shelter you need to protect your support equipment and add more when you can.

POOL HOUSES AND CHANGING ROOMS

The queen of water-side structures is the pool owner's version of a dream house: a full-blown pool house complete with wet bar, kitchen, bathroom, and maybe even a guest room or two. But just a shed big enough to allow a quick change of clothes will save you from a summer-long parade of people in wet bathing suits traipsing through your house. In the mid-range there are myriad choices that give you sheltered space for entertaining, changing, or waiting out a sudden change in the weather.

Here's a dream come true for those who never want to venture far from the pool: a changing pavilion, complete outdoor kitchen, and even an open-air living room.

This pool house, with the air of a fairy-tale cottage, has all the comforts of home—and enough space to store a full complement of pool-support gear and sports equipment.

With this rustic shower stall just inches away from the spa, a pre-soak shower takes only seconds. What's more, it eliminates the need to trek through the house in a wet bathing suit.

time-saving tip

To avoid unpleasant (and possibly expensive) surprises, check your town's zoning requirements before you build any pool structure, even if it's a pre-fab storage shed.

The arbor above, unadorned by plants on top, casts ever-changing shadows on the white wall behind it. The result is an air of cool, elegant simplicity.

A long pergola (right) provides a shady spot for al fresco dining and for watching the action in the pool from the comfort of a well-cushioned chaise.

ARBORS AND PERGOLAS

These structures, which are designed to provide relief from the sun's heat, can be just large enough to shelter a table for two, spacious enough to cover a large deck, or any size in between. Regardless of size or style, an arbor or a pergola not only gives you a shady place to relax or party but can also solve the nagging problem of how to screen your site from above—for instance, to block the view from the windows of your neighbors' houses or a nearby apartment building.

Often, visual intrusions come from above—for instance, the windows of a nearby house or a roadway that overlooks your property. When that's the case, erecting an arbor, like the one over this spa, is a simple and effective way to gain privacy.

164

building an arbor or a pergola

The terms *arbor* and *pergola* are often used interchangeably, but there is a minor distinction between the two. Although both consist of posts supporting an open roof of beams or lattice, an arbor is broader and may be connected to a building on one side. A pergola, on the other hand, is always freestanding and narrow. Regardless of which of these shade-giving structures you choose to build, the technique is the same. This project is best done with two people. As with any permanent structure, consult your local building department before proceeding.

MATERIALS LIST

- 6-by-6 posts
- One post base and anchor bolt for each post (if you are affixing to concrete) *or* one precast concrete pier with post base, plus concrete mix (if building on soil)
- Galvanized nails
- One ½-by-10" lag bolt with washer per post
- Two ½-by-7" lag bolts with washers per beam
- Braces and wooden stakes
- Two 6-by-6 beams
- 4-by-4 rafters

1 Fasten each post base to the concrete with an anchor bolt (if building on the ground, dig a post hole, fill with concrete, and position the top of the precast pier 3 to 4 inches above grade level). Cut the posts to length if necessary. Nail the posts to the post bases.

2 Use a level on two adjacent sides to check that each post is vertical. Secure it in position with temporary braces nailed to wooden stakes that are driven into the ground.

3 With a helper, position a beam on top of the posts. Check that the posts are still vertical and the beam is level. Use a ⁷⁄₁₆-inch bit to drill a 9-inch-deep hole down through the beam into each post. With a wrench, install a 10-inch lag bolt into the hole. Repeat for the other beam.

4 Set and space the rafters on top of the beams. With a ⁷⁄₁₆-inch bit, drill 6-inch-deep holes through the rafters and into the beams. Install a 7-inch lag bolt into each hole. For more strength, you can install diagonal bracing between the posts and the beams. For shade, cover the rafters with vines or lath, either 1 by 2s or 2 by 2s.

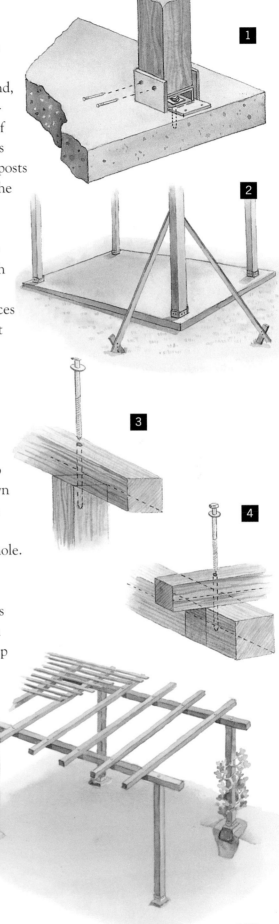

CABANAS AND GAZEBOS

Cabanas and gazebos are the landscaping equivalent to grandstands: they give you a sheltered place to sit and watch the action at poolside. Generally speaking, a cabana (the name comes from the Spanish word for "hut") has a solid roof, three lightweight walls, and one open side facing the object of your viewing pleasure—in this case, your pool. Gazebos have been standard features in English gardens since the 1600s and have gained widespread popularity in this country in the past decade or so. They are open on all sides, allowing those inside to sit and look across the landscape (the name may be a combination of the words "gaze" and "about").

SAUNAS

For increasing numbers of people, a sauna and a pool are a match made in heaven. Your sauna can be a freestanding structure, or it can be incorporated into a pool

A pool that's surrounded by a striking landscape deserves a classic gazebo. From this roofed but wide-open perch, no part of the scenery can escape the attention of admiring viewers.

house, garage, or basement. For more about saunas, including how to build your own, see pages 210 to 217.

STORAGE STRUCTURES

Although other pool-side structures are nice extras, sheltered storage space is a must. You'll need a fair amount of it, too, for the vacuum, leaf skimmer, brushes, chemicals, and other pool equipment. Storing all those necessities in a covered, well-ventilated area will not only keep them out of sight but also prolong their life. Most likely you will also need room to store outdoor furniture, play and fitness gear, and other accessories when they're not in use.

A long portico frames a view of the pool and the cove beyond. It also offers handy refuge for pool-side loungers when rain clouds open up.

customizing a prefab storage shed

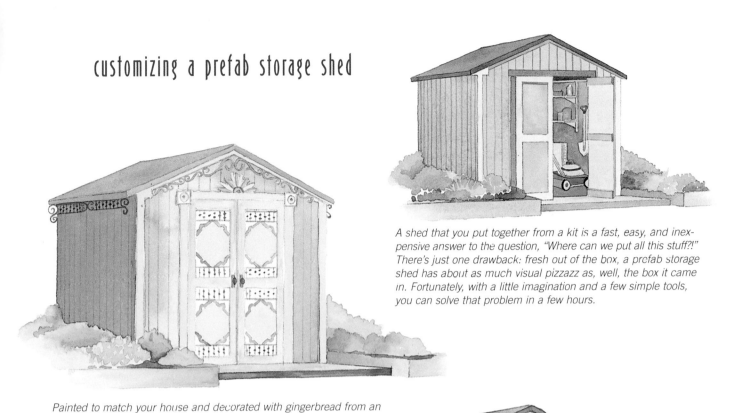

A shed that you put together from a kit is a fast, easy, and inexpensive answer to the question, "Where can we put all this stuff?!" There's just one drawback: fresh out of the box, a prefab storage shed has about as much visual pizzazz as, well, the box it came in. Fortunately, with a little imagination and a few simple tools, you can solve that problem in a few hours.

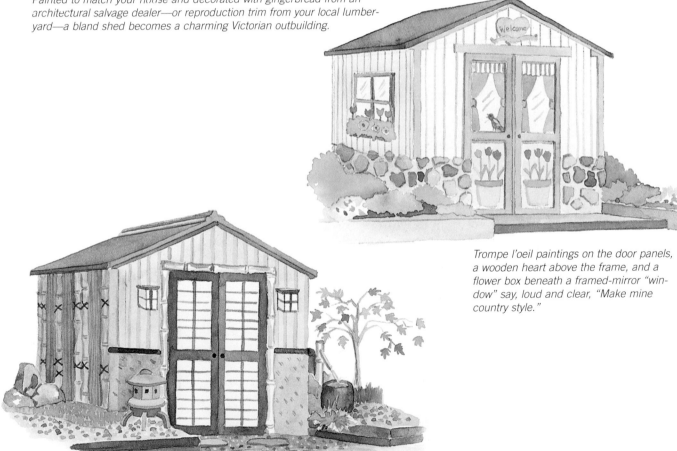

Painted to match your house and decorated with gingerbread from an architectural salvage dealer—or reproduction trim from your local lumberyard—a bland shed becomes a charming Victorian outbuilding.

Trompe l'oeil paintings on the door panels, a wooden heart above the frame, and a flower box beneath a framed-mirror "window" say, loud and clear, "Make mine country style."

If yours is an Asian-inspired landscape, adorn your shed with willow or bamboo panels and surround it with rock constructions, stone lanterns, and bamboo and stone fountains.

water on water

The sight, sound, and feel of moving water can relax our bodies, inspire our minds, and restore our spirits. In a pool setting, a water feature can also mask the sounds of traffic and neighbors, cast a magical aura over nighttime gatherings, and make children (and grownups) shriek with glee as they hurtle down

a water slide. As with all the other elements in your landscape, you will want to select water features that complement the style of your pool and its surroundings, and suit your taste, budget, and the way you use your pool.

WATERFALLS

Whether you have a waterfall installed at the time your pool is built or add one later, you have an enormous range of styles and effects from which to choose. You can simulate the look and sound of the real thing, with water cascading over time-worn boulders, either real or synthetic. Or you can abandon all pretense in favor of a simple sheet of water flowing over marble, stone, or concrete.

In this setting (left), water tumbles down a rocky slope. At the bottom it forks into two waterfalls, one emptying into the spa, the other into the pool.

The owners of the pool below spared no effort to mimic a natural pond. At one end, water cascades from gaps between artfully placed boulders.

When the time came to refurbish this pool (see also page 146), the owners were fortunate: the retaining wall that held back a sizable hillside was rock solid. All it required was a coat of stucco to cover the painted brick, followed by ceramic tile.

Newly tiled and with the original iron railing gone from the top, the wall forms an elegant backdrop for water-spewing lions. On the slope behind the pool, low-maintenance native plants replace a landscape that demanded considerable upkeep—and a lot of irrigation.

Hidden behind the retaining wall is plumbing that connects the fountains to the pool's circulation system (above). Whether installed when a pool is built or later on, this kind of work demands the services of a professional plumber or pool technician.

FOUNTAINS

Of all water features, a fountain is the easiest to add because you already have the essentials in place: pumps and access to the electricity powering the pool equipment. You can buy ready-made fountains in nurseries, garden shops, and home centers; seek out a hand-made original in craft galleries; or make your own.

Anything that spouts water will do the job, from an antique urn to a rock with a hole drilled in it. Whichever spouting device you choose, though, fountains that function in conjunction with swimming pools fall into three basic categories: fountainheads installed inside the pool, fixtures that sit on or under the coping and shoot water into the pool,

and wall-mounted fountains that spill into the pool. All are best installed at the time the pool is constructed, but can be added later. In almost every case you'll need the help of a professional pool technician. If you want to simply enjoy the sight and sound of moving water, you can easily make a freestanding or wall-mounted self-contained fountain.

the pool by night

If you routinely take nocturnal dips, throw frequent evening pool parties, or simply exult in the play of light on water, the illumination of your pool is a major aesthetic consideration. But even if you rarely glance out the window after dark, good lighting is a must from a safety standpoint. Check with your town's building department and your insurance company about guidelines that may mandate certain types or levels of lighting.

design tip

Not sure where you need light? Experiment with inexpensive clip-on lamps that you can buy at your local hardware store. Just plug them into outdoor-grade extension cords and fasten them to tree limbs or fences, or ask a helper to hold them aloft as you ponder the placement possibilities.

What appears to be an underwater meteor shower (or maybe millions of aquatic lightning bugs) is actually more than 2,000 fiber-optic lights.

LIVING IN THE LIGHT

Good outdoor lighting is both functional and aesthetically pleasing. On the practical side, it offers the right kind of light when and where you need it for entertaining, al fresco cooking or dining, or just relaxing. At the same time, judicious lighting adds to the aura of your pool or spa by highlighting architectural features and plantings or by casting a magical glow on the water—viewed from indoors or out.

When a pool occupies a setting as dramatic as this one, getting the lighting just right can be tricky. Here, strategically placed fixtures provide safe illumination for twilight swimming (or cocktail get-togethers). But the glow doesn't obstruct the breathtaking sunset.

LIGHTING OPTIONS

A traditional 120-volt outdoor lighting system requires buried, waterproof pipes that meet local safety codes. That can translate into a long wait for a busy electrician, followed by a large bill for services. Fortunately, you have a faster and far less expensive option: low-voltage outdoor lighting, which uses only 12 volts of electricity. The easy part is installing a transformer that steps down the voltage from 120 to 12. The hard part is deciding where you want to place your lights, the kind of effect you want to achieve, and which of the multitude of available fixtures you want to use.

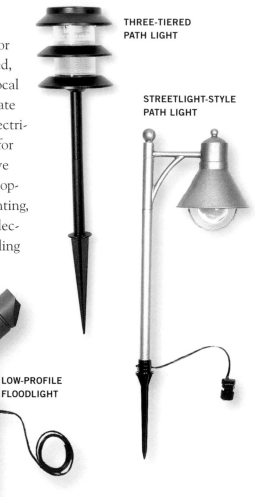

THREE-TIERED PATH LIGHT

STREETLIGHT-STYLE PATH LIGHT

LOW-PROFILE FLOODLIGHT

POST CAP LIGHT

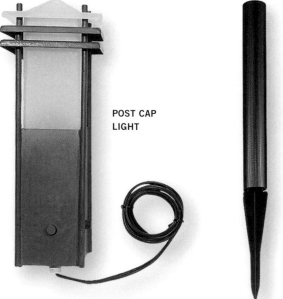

SOLAR LIGHT WITH INSTALLATION HARDWARE

LET THERE BE LIGHT

Building-supply stores sell attractive low-voltage lighting kits that are a snap to install, even if the extent of your electrical expertise is flicking a circuit breaker from off to on. You'll need to plug the transformer into a properly installed GFCI-protected outdoor outlet; if you don't have one, a professional electrician can easily install it. Lay out the wire in a direct route, following the manufacturer's directions. Don't let the wire cross over itself, and avoid tight, twisty turns. Be sure not to add more lights than the kit's maker prescribes.

MATERIALS LIST

- Low-voltage lighting kit
- Measuring tape
- Pliers
- Insulated screwdriver
- Wire cutter with stripper
- Shovel
- Twine, garden hose, lime, or flour (for marking route)

Light different points of interest, as well as pathways and stairways, to provide safety and enhance the appeal of the pool at night.

1 Lay out the route you want your lights to illuminate. You can snake twine or a garden hose on the ground, or simply sprinkle lime or white flour along the desired path. Then dig a trench at least 6 inches deep following the outline.

2 Position the light fixtures along the route beside the trench. Lay the low-voltage cable in the trench and clip the wire leads extending from each light fixture to the cable. Some types of lights screw to the cable, rather than clipping.

3 Drive the attached ground spikes into the soil. Cover the cable with mulch or soil.

4 Near the GFCI receptacle and in a spot not likely to be bumped, mount the transformer with screws drilled into a stable surface. Following the manufacturer's directions, connect the wires to the transformer, using an insulated screwdriver.

5 Plug the transformer into a GFCI-protected outlet. Adjust the settings to turn the lights on and off automatically at particular times of day.

the finishing touches

In the last few decades, open-air living has become a national pastime—even if, in many places, it's only possible for two or three months of the year. The popularity of hosting meals and parties al fresco has spawned a huge range of furniture and accessories designed for outdoor use. When you're faced with the decision of what to buy for your pool or spa setting, the choices can be mind-boggling, but they needn't be.

A tile-topped trunk does double duty as a storage unit and cocktail table.

Thick cushions top a bench made from the same stone that surrounds the pool.

FURNITURE SHOPPING

Regardless of whether you need enough furniture to accommodate several dozen partygoers or just a table and chairs for two, there are four considerations worth bearing in mind: style, size, durability, and—most important of all—comfort. Before you purchase any furniture, try it out. Recline in the lounge chairs, pull the dining chairs up to the table, settle into the easy chairs, and put your feet up on the ottomans. If the people in your household vary greatly in stature, have them "test drive" the pieces, too. It's rare that one size fits all, so you may want to buy chairs or benches in several different sizes, even if they don't exactly match.

ACCESSORIES

In your poolscape, accessories function just as they do inside your home: they help you turn a pleasant but bland space into one that says, "This is mine!" There are no rules for choosing pool-side decor, but bear in mind that more is not better. Too many objects near the pool can pose dangers to people moving about the deck.

Candles, in holders hung from metal poles, illuminate these garden paths at night. By day, they become distinctive decorative accessories.

Packed with bright annuals, a hand-made wooden planter makes a colorful, personal statement at poolside.

In this small pool area, art doubles as seating in the form of a bench by ceramic artist Pedro Castillo.

One or two outstanding pieces, placed at a safe distance from the water, will add visual pizzazz without putting swimmers at risk. If space is tight, look for objects that are useful as well as decorative— for instance, a quirky folk art sculpture that can double as a towel rack, a bench that's also a work of art, or a one-of-a-kind planter.

sanitizing the water

Disease-carrying microorganisms and algae thrive in water—particularly in the heated water of spas—so regular sanitizing is essential. Techniques range from the traditional practice of adding chlorine to newer technology that requires almost no chemicals to do the job.

HOW CHLORINATION WORKS

Chlorine is the most popular choice for controlling pathogens in pool water. Not only does it kill algae and bacteria, it also breaks down organic debris by oxidizing it. Chlorine is available

in three forms: liquid, which is rarely used for residential pools; granular, which is dissolved in water before being added; and slow-dissolving tablets, which are placed in a floating feeder that gradually releases chlorine into the water.

No matter which form you use, the chlorine reacts with your pool or spa water to produce, among other substances, hypochlorous acid. This compound, also referred to as free chlorine, is what actually does the sanitizing. However, hypochlorous acid degrades fairly quickly when exposed to sunlight. To counteract this, a stabilizing agent, most often cyanuric acid, is typically added to the water along with chlorine.

To determine if your water needs chlorination, test the chlorine level a few times a week using a test kit from a pool-supply store. (Buy a kit that also measures pH level, total alkalinity, and calcium hardness, all discussed on the following pages.) The amount of free chlorine should be 1.0 to 2.0 parts per million (ppm).

The exact amount of chlorine to add to your pool depends on multiple factors, including the brand and how heavily your pool is used. In general, expect your pool or spa to need a daily dose of chlorine during periods of heavy use. Be sure to follow the package directions carefully.

Clear water, such as in this pristine pool, looks deceptively natural. Maintaining it, however, is the result of careful chemistry.

CHLORINE'S SHORTCOMINGS

As hypochlorous acid encounters ammonia or nitrogen in the water—introduced by swimmers in the form of perspiration, saliva, and urine—it oxidizes those compounds, leaving behind chloramines. Chloramines have little capacity to further sanitize the water, and they can actually be an irritant. When a pool has a strong "chlorine" smell or stings swimmers' eyes, it's usually a sign of too *little* free chlorine. The cure is superchlorination, also known as a shock treatment—a high dose of chlorine added to the water to break down chloramines. You'll know it's time to superchlorinate when a strong smell becomes evident, or when ordinary chlorination does not clear the water.

"SHOCKING" THE POOL

A shock treatment is something you can administer on your own, using a chemical shocker (also called an oxidizer or burner). It usually comes in the form of a powder that's sprinkled into the water. You'll typically need to shock the pool about once a week during the swimming season—more frequently if the pool is used heavily.

Different shockers release different amounts of available chlorine to do the job, so check the instructions on the package. Also make sure the pump and filter are turned on. Keep everyone out of the pool for several hours after a shock treatment; it takes that long for the chlorine level to return to normal.

adding chemicals safely

■ ■ ■

Pool chemicals can be extremely corrosive, posing a threat not only to the lining of the pool or spa but to the person adding them. In most cases, you will need to add chemicals manually—therefore, very carefully. Be sure to protect your eyes and hands.

To add granular chemicals, mix them first in a bucket by adding the granules to the water; never pour water on top of granules because they are likely to splash out and can cause serious injury. Pour the resulting liquid into the pool at various points, pouring close to the surface to minimize splashing. Add liquid chemicals the same way. To add large tablets, simply place them in a feeder.

THE SALT ADVANTAGE

The chemicals that are used to chlorinate a pool or spa warrant careful handling, since they can be extremely hazardous. One recent advance eliminates that danger by deriving chlorine from ordinary table salt—sodium chloride—that's periodically added to the pool water. The device, a chlorine generator, creates an electric current that splits salt molecules and releases chloride ions into the water.

Chlorine generators can be used for large in-ground pools, as well as above-ground pools and spas. The amount of salt required will depend on the size and location of your pool and the specific chlorine generator. But even when a seemingly large amount of salt is needed, it's relatively low compared to the salt in seawater—which means the water won't taste salty.

A pool or spa with a chlorine generator will still need periodic shocking with high levels of chlorine to keep the water clear. Some types of chlorine generators have a large enough capacity to produce these high levels themselves. A dial is simply set to "shock," and the generator does the work. Others, though, are not large enough to handle this task and require chlorine to be added separately when the quantity of chloramines is too high. (The addition of chlorine to the pool or spa will not interfere with the production of chlorine by the generator.)

Instead of adding pure chlorine to the water, you can sanitize your pool in creative ways. A chlorine generator, left, releases chlorine when ordinary salt is added to the water; a floating ionizer, above, uses a solar-generated electrical current to release small amounts of algae- and bacteria-fighting minerals.

THE BROMINE ALTERNATIVE

Chemically similar to chlorine, bromine has become a popular alternative for sanitizing indoor pools and spas. (It's not a viable option for outdoor pools because it breaks down quickly in the presence of sunlight.) Bromine kills pathogens via oxidation, the same way that chlorine does. However, bromine combines with organic matter to form bromamines rather than chloramines; bromamines do not produce the same acrid smell that chloramines do and are less noxious to the eyes and skin. Bromamines break down by natural processes, so there is no need to perform shock treatment.

SOLAR IONIZATION

One method of water purification that is gaining popularity is solar ionization. Borrowing a technique from ancient Rome, where metal coins were used to keep water fresh, a solar ionizer releases trace amounts of copper and silver into the surrounding water to combat algae and bacteria. The device uses solar energy to generate a small electrical current, which in turn powers a specially alloyed mineral electrode. The amount of

mineral ions released into the water poses no danger and falls within drinking-water standards defined by the Environmental Protection Agency.

Solar ionization doesn't completely eliminate the need for chlorine, since some pool and spa contaminants—such as dust, sunscreen, or body oils—are unaffected by mineral ions and can cloud the water. You'll need to add a small amount of chlorine or other oxidizer occasionally, but you can expect a solar ionizer to reduce the amount of chlorine you use by about 80 percent on average.

safety tip

To prevent dangerous chemical reactions, never mix different types of pool chemicals together before adding them to the water—even if they are different formulations of the same additive, such as chlorine.

balancing the water

Proper chlorination is just one part of keeping pool and spa water healthy. Equally important is maintaining an optimum chemical balance: pH, total alkalinity, calcium hardness, and total dissolved solids. Otherwise, the water can damage the pool or spa and cause discomfort for bathers.

UNDERSTANDING pH

Put simply, a liquid's pH is a measure of its overall acid-alkalinity balance. Water that is too acidic may corrode metal equipment, deteriorate surface materials such as plaster coatings and vinyl liners, and cause skin irritation and sore throats. If the water is too alkaline, it can cause scale to form on pool walls and plumbing equipment and can cloud the water. To make matters worse, both high acidity and high alkalinity undermine chlorine's effectiveness in killing microorganisms.

A liquid's pH is measured on a scale of 0 to 14, with a value of 0 indicating extreme acidity and a reading of 14 indicating extreme alkalinity. A pH of 7 denotes a neutral state in which acidity and alkalinity are perfectly balanced. The ideal pH for a pool or spa lies between 7.2 and 7.8.

TESTING AND ADJUSTING It's simple to measure your water's pH using a test kit from a pool-supply store. Special paper strips change color when you dampen them with a drop of pool or spa water. Matching the strips against a color chart yields a reading.

If the reading lies outside the optimum range, you will need to adjust the pH by adding either an acidic or an alkaline substance. For a pH below 7.2, add sodium carbonate, known as soda ash, or sodium bicarbonate, which is ordinary baking soda. If the pH is above 7.8, add muriatic acid or sodium bisulfate to lower it. The exact amount of treatment to add and the method for adding it will vary, so be sure to check labels.

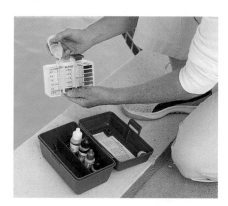

Keeping pool and spa water clean and fresh requires ongoing monitoring using a simple test kit, such as the one at left.

how often to test

MEASUREMENT	POOL	STANDALONE SPA
Free chlorine	Once or twice a week	Twice a week
pH	Once a week	Twice a week
Total alkalinity	Once a week	Twice a week
Calcium hardness	At the start of the season	Once after each filling
Total dissolved solids	At the start of the season	Every two to three months, depending on use

TOTAL ALKALINITY

Although this component of water chemistry is closely related to pH, the two are subtly—and importantly—different. Total alkalinity (TA) is a measure of the quantity of alkaline material in water, regardless of whether it's balanced by an equal quantity of acidic material. Therefore, two samples of water that have a pH of 7.2 can differ in their total TA.

The ideal TA is between 80 and 150 parts per million (ppm), depending on the type of pool: for plaster-coated gunite pools the number should tend toward the low end of the spectrum, from 80 to 125 ppm; for vinyl, fiberglass, and painted-plaster surfaces it should tend toward the upper end, from 125 to 150 ppm. A TA that's too low can lead to rapid fluctuations in the water's pH, sometimes described as the water having no buffering capability. A TA that's too high makes it difficult to correct or adjust the

cost-saving tip

When adding chemicals—whether to increase the chlorine level or to adjust the pH—it's best to add a little at a time and check the effect, especially with spas, where only a small amount of chemicals can change the balance. Proceeding cautiously will save chemicals as well as money. You can always add more if necessary.

While the work required to balance the water in a pool or spa may seem a bit complex, the end result—such as this enticingly beautiful cascade—makes it worth the effort.

pH—the water is too buffered. It's important to have the right amount of buffering in your pool so you can adjust the pH as well as avoid rapid fluctuations.

A test kit contains stoppered bottles for collecting water samples, along with tablets to dissolve in the water. The number of tablets required to change the water from yellow to pink indicates the total alkalinity in parts per million. To guarantee proper readings, it's essential to keep the sample vials clean and free of contamination. Plunge a test vial under the water with the cap on. Remove the cap, fill the vial with water, then screw the cap back in place underwater. This assures that the sample taken isn't affected by debris floating on the surface. Above all, do not cover the opening of the vial with your finger; instead, use the cap. Oils and acids from your skin can alter the results.

ideal levels

MEASUREMENT	OPTIMUM READING
Free chlorine	1.0 to 2.0 ppm
pH	7.2 to 7.8
Total alkalinity	80 to 125 ppm (for gunite)
	125 to 150 (for vinyl, fiberglass, and painted plaster)
Total dissolved solids	Not to exceed 2,500 ppm
Calcium hardness	200 to 400 ppm

If the TA is too high, you can lower it with muriatic acid; if it's too low, use sodium bicarbonate—baking soda—or chemicals found in pool-supply stores.

To determine how much muriatic acid to add, you'll first need to know your pool's volume (see page 91). Divide the volume in gallons by 125,000, then multiply by the number of parts per million change desired; this provides the amount of muriatic acid in quarts. If, for instance, your pool holds 10,000 gallons, and you want to decrease total alkalinity by 20 ppm, you would need to add 1.6 quarts of muriatic acid (10,000 ÷ 125,000 = .08 quarts for each ppm decrease; × 20 for 20 ppm = 1.6). To determine how much sodium bicarbonate to add, the rule is that each increase of 10 ppm requires .14 pounds of bicarbonate for every 1,000 gallons. To raise the alkalinity 20 ppm in a 10,000-gallon pool, for example, you would add 2.80 pounds of sodium bicarbonate (.14 × 10 = 1.40 pounds for each 10 ppm increase; × 2 for 20 ppm = 2.80 pounds).

CALCIUM HARDNESS

Water is often described as hard or soft. The terms refer to the amount of dissolved minerals it contains. Hard water contains more minerals—of which calcium is the most common—while soft water contains fewer.

Where pools and spas are concerned, water that is too hard can turn cloudy, have an elevated pH, and cause calcium scales to form. (High water temperatures also encourage scaling.) Water that's too soft can soften or etch plaster, causing tile grout to dissolve and tiles to pop off, and create cracks in vinyl liners. Not all test kits measure calcium levels, although the more sophisticated ones do. If yours doesn't, you can take a sample of water to a pool store for testing.

In most cases, the calcium ion content of water should be maintained between 200 and 400 ppm. To increase the water's hardness —that is, to add more calcium ions—mix the chemical chloride dihydrate into the water at a rate of .1 pound for every 2,500 gallons. Decreasing hardness is more difficult. The most effective way is to drain some of the water from the pool and dilute what remains with softer water. A pro-

fessional can also filter the calcium ions from the water with a nano-filter, which can remove the most minute particles imaginable. Another, less effective way to lower calcium levels is by adding sodium hexametaphosphate, which causes the calcium to react and form particles that can be trapped by the pool's filtration system.

TOTAL DISSOLVED SOLIDS

Total dissolved solids, or TDS, is a measure of everything dissolved in water, including chemicals, minerals, residue from bathers (such as sunscreen), and all other impurities. These inert substances become more concentrated as water evaporates, resulting, over time, in cloudy water. The accumulation of TDS also causes sanitizers to become less effective, increasing the likelihood of algae growth, scaling, staining, and corrosion.

A TDS meter lets you monitor the level easily. You can also take a sample of water to a pool store to have it measured. To avoid elevated TDS levels (higher than 2,500 ppm), you can regularly add alum-based clarifiers, such as aluminum sulphate or sodium bisulphate (also known as dry acid), to your pool or spa. An even better approach is to periodically drain the pool a few inches and add fresh water.

If the TDS density reaches 2,500 ppm, more drastic action needs to be taken. Drain the pool or spa completely, then refill with fresh water. In a heavily used swimming pool, you might have to do this every three or four years. By contrast, a 300-gallon spa used by two people per day would reach TDS overload in just 50 days of use.

AN INDEX FOR OVERALL BALANCE

Even if pH, TA, calcium hardness, and TDS all fall within recommended limits, the water in a pool or spa may still cause scaling or corrosion. If this is the case, it may help to have a pool professional consult an overall indicator of water balance known as the Langelier Saturation Index.

This table considers all factors that are involved in balancing water and makes recommendations for specific adjustments to bring the water into balance. A well-balanced pool has a reading of 0 on the saturation index. If the reading is negative, the water is likely to be corrosive; if it's positive, the water is likely to cause scaling.

smart tip

Always adjust total alkalinity before you adjust pH, because once TA is in the proper range, the pH will be more stable, requiring only minimal adjustments.

care and maintenance

For the most part, tending your pool or spa entails just simple cleaning and upkeep. Sometimes, however, problems occur, ranging from murky water to noisy pumps. Often you'll be able to handle these situations on your own, but for some of the larger, more technical repairs you'll need professional help.

cleaning your pool

Keeping the interior of your swimming pool fresh and clean doesn't demand intensive labor, but it does take a steady commitment. Expect to spend between four and eight hours each week during the peak season—a small outlay compared to the amount of time you'll spend enjoying your pool.

THE BEST TOOLS FOR THE JOB

Using the right tools will make cleaning your pool easier and faster. You'll find these at any large pool-supply retailer.

LEAF SKIMMER This long-handled net is a must for removing large pieces of floating debris.

VACUUM Another weapon that's essential in any cleaning arsenal, a vacuum either connects to a pool's circulation system or has its own power supply. Vacuums suction out dirt that has settled to the bottom.

WALL AND FLOOR BRUSH
This nylon-bristle brush cleans the walls and floor of vinyl, fiberglass, and painted pools.

ALGAE BRUSH
Concrete pools may require one of these; its stainless-steel bristles are up to the challenge of cleaning plaster walls.

TILE BRUSH If your pool has tiled walls, a handheld tile brush is great for removing calcium scale and other deposits without harming the grout. Use a pumice stone for stubborn spots on tile.

quick tip

One of the easiest ways to keep a pool fresh is to clean it at least a little bit after each use—perhaps leaf skimming, vacuuming, or brushing. By breaking maintenance tasks into daily chores—rather than weekly workloads—you're more likely to keep on top of them.

SKIMMING DEBRIS

Skimming by hand is one of the quickest and most effective ways to keep a pool clean. A few simple swipes will remove floating objects such as leaves before they sink to the bottom, greatly increasing the efficiency of the pool's circulation system and reducing the need for chlorine.

A long-handled skimmer makes it easy to remove leaves and other floating debris from the water.

CLEANING OUT THE BASKETS

Keeping the strainer baskets clear will also boost the efficiency of the circulation system, resulting in a much cleaner pool. Remove leaves and anything else that could obstruct the water flow at least once a week, especially if your vacuum is connected to the mechanical skimmer. Strainer baskets may be in the pool deck or, for an above-ground pool, attached to the side.

VACUUMING

Vacuuming every week helps keep the water clear and reduces the need to add sanitizing chemicals. Vacuums come in many designs and styles (see page 96). All manual vacuums should be worked back and forth across the swimming pool, overlapping slightly on each stroke. Depending on the amount of dirt in the pool, it may be necessary to clean the filter each time you vacuum.

The skimmer basket is located in the pool deck and traps floating debris. It needs to be cleaned out often—every day during periods of heavy use—to keep the pool filter functioning at maximum capacity.

CLEANING THE WALLS

Brushing the pool walls at least once a week helps eliminate everything from calcium scale to algae buildup before they start to become serious problems. You can use a stiff brush on a plaster-lined concrete pool, but fiberglass and vinyl pools require a softer brush.

For tiles, be sure not to use anything too abrasive or stiff—it can scratch the tiles or destroy the grout. Water-line tile scum can be removed with a nonabrasive chlorine-based liquid and a tile brush or a sponge. For tough spots, use a nylon scouring pad or a pumice stone, which works like a giant eraser. Whatever type of pool you have, make sure to use a cleaner recommended by the pool manufacturer.

before the first swim
■ ■ ■

Tempting as it is to plunge into your pool the moment construction is complete, you need to clean and balance the water first. New pools, whether fiberglass, vinyl lined, or concrete, invariably contain dust and other dirt that needs to be eliminated. To do this, run the pool's filter continuously, 24 hours a day, until the water is clear; this may take anywhere from a day or two to an entire week or more. Periodically, you will need to stop and clear the filter (see page 193) so the purification process will be successful.

Plaster-coated gunite and shotcrete pools pose an additional challenge: the wet plaster often turns the water murky. Handling this will require more time, and will also require you to keep a closer eye on the filter, which will need more frequent cleaning. After the water is clear, reduce the filtration time by one hour a day until clarity is achieved. Then balance the pH, total alkalinity, and other factors of water chemistry (see pages 182 to 185). When the water is balanced, add a sanitizer such as chlorine—and then start swimming.

cleaning your spa

Because of their exceedingly high water temperatures as well as the heavy use they get, spas tend to require frequent maintenance to keep them clean.

THE BEST TOOLS FOR THE JOB

The best tools for keeping a spa clean are basically the same as those used to clean swimming pools—just on a smaller scale.

LEAF SKIMMER As in a pool, this long-handled net is necessary for removing large pieces of floating debris.

VACUUM A spa vacuum can be powered in several ways. If your spa is not connected to the circulation system of an in-ground pool, a good solution is a vacuum that's powered by a jet of water from a garden hose.

SPA WAND A more stream-lined alternative to a vacuum, a spa wand also collects debris through suction. It may be powered either by pumping or turning the handle or by a rechargeable battery. A spa wand is also handy for cleaning pool steps.

BUCKET AND SOFT SPONGE These two low-tech tools are a must for cleaning interior spa walls.

SKIMMING AND VACUUMING

Since a spa is so small, even a minimal amount of debris can lower the efficiency of the circulation system. Bring out the skimmer each time you use your spa. In addition, either vacuum or use a spa wand twice a week to remove litter that has settled to the bottom.

CLEANING OUT THE BASKETS

Debris-free baskets are essential to the proper operation of the circulation system. Clean the skimmers twice a week by removing leaves and anything else obstructing the water flow. With in-ground spas, the strainer baskets are hidden in the surrounding deck; for portable spas, the baskets are near the pump.

CLEANING THE INNER SURFACE

Because total dissolved solids (see page 185) build up quickly, spa water needs to be drained fairly often. Emptying the spa provides an opportunity for cleaning the inner surfaces. Brush the spa interior to eliminate calcium scales and any algae buildup. A plaster-lined concrete spa can withstand stiff brushing, but fiberglass and acrylic spas are more delicate.

To clean tile, don't use anything very abrasive or stiff that could scratch the tile and destroy the grout. A pumice stone works well, removing scale like a giant eraser. A putty knife is also great for scraping off especially heavy scale. Another alternative is to dissolve the scale with a 50-50 mix of water and muriatic acid; apply it with a nylon brush and start scrubbing (see safety tip above). Rinse well when you're finished.

Even an indoor spa, which doesn't collect leaves or other garden debris, needs regular cleaning to keep the water sparkling.

equipment maintenance

Just like a pool or spa's shell, the mechanical equipment that keeps everything running efficiently will benefit from regular maintenance. Most of these chores are simple, and if you perform them regularly—and understand the basic workings of the equipment—you'll be able to spot and handle small problems before they turn into big ones.

THE PUMP

The pump for a pool or spa requires very little maintenance. Pumps are generally self-priming—meaning they don't have to be filled with water before you turn them on at the start of the season. But you'll need to regularly clean out the strainer basket inside, in most cases once a week. To get to the basket, remove the top of the pump housing; refer to the owner's manual to determine the specific location of your pump's basket.

While you're checking the basket, take a moment to inspect the condition of the O-ring or gasket that seals the lid of the pump housing. If it is cracked or has deteriorated, replace it; otherwise, the lid won't be able to form the seal that's needed to keep the pump in operation.

Serious pump problems, such as an obvious water leak, will require professional help.

Periodic care of a pool's mechanical equipment will keep everything running smoothly and head off potential problems before they arise.

cleaning the filter

TYPE	FREQUENCY	TECHNIQUE
Cartridge	Every three to four months	Turn off the pump. Remove the filter, hose it off, and soak it in detergent according to the manufacturer's instructions for removing oils.
Sand	Every month	Turn off the pump. Circulate water through the filter in the reverse direction for about 10 minutes, a process known as backwashing.
Diatomaceous earth	Every three to four months	Turn off the pump. Backwash the filter (see above), then add more diatomaceous earth to the skimmers. Water will carry the D.E. to the filter and recoat it.

THE FILTER

No matter which type of filter you have in your pool or spa—cartridge, sand, or diatomaceous earth—it will need periodic cleaning to keep the water clear. Depending on the type of filter and how heavily you use your pool or spa, filter cleaning frequency can range anywhere from once a month to three or four times each year.

Contrary to what you might expect, cleaning the filter more often than that doesn't help. In fact it hinders the filtration process. That's because a slightly dirty filter is actually more efficient than a perfectly clean one. The particles of dirt lodged in it help trap additional particles, removing debris from the water more quickly.

Ideally, the filter should be cleaned before any deterioration in water quality is noticeable. To avoid having any problems, check the pressure gauge and the flow meter in the pool—one is positioned on the line into the filter, the other on the return line out of the filter. As the filter becomes dirty, the difference in flow between the gauges will increase. When the difference reaches 10 to 15 pounds per square inch, it's time to clean the filter. (See the above chart for general cleaning advice; follow the manufacturer's instructions for more specifics.)

THE HEATER

Of all the equipment connected to a pool or spa, the heater requires the least maintenance. Gas heaters, for instance, can usually go for a year or two—sometimes longer—before they need professional servicing, and electric heaters can go longer still. With either type, check the manufacturer's recommendations.

If the heater doesn't warm up the water, calcium scales might be building up in its tubes, restricting the flow. To solve the problem, have a professional disassemble the heater and clean out the tubes using acid or a wire brush.

hiring a pool service

Many homeowners opt to hire a pool service to do all or some of the work of maintaining a swimming pool or spa. This may include balancing the water, vacuuming the pool, cleaning the skimmer baskets as well as the strainer basket in the pump, and checking the condition of the filter.

The cost runs from $100 or more per month for weekly visits, depending on location. Even if you use a pool service, you'll still need to empty the skimmer baskets between visits and keep up regular hand skimming.

troubleshooting common problems

Even with diligent maintenance of your pool or spa, issues will occasionally arise. The problems listed below are among the most common. Most of them can be handled by homeowners.

pool or spa shell

PROBLEM	POSSIBLE CAUSE	SOLUTION
Loss of grouting in tiled pools or spas	Soft water, which has low calcium levels, and can sometimes dissolve the calcium in grouting	Regrout the pool and test the calcium levels in the water. If it's lower than 250 ppm, add calcium chloride.
Rough, scaly surfaces	Incorrect balance among pH, total alkalinity, and calcium hardness	Test for pH, total alkalinity, and calcium hardness and bring the levels within recommended parameters. A pool-supply store can conduct a Langelier water-balance test (see page 185) to advise you further.
Slippery surfaces	An algae colony, which may have formed because of insufficient chlorination or dead spots in water circulation	Use a brush on the slippery area to remove as much algae as possible, then superchlorinate (see page 179). An algicide may be needed to prevent a recurrence.
Tide mark at the water line	Build-up of greasy deposits, such as suntan lotion and cosmetics	Brush the area using a cleanser recommended by a pool-supply store; be sure it will not react with chlorine in the water.

filter and pump

PROBLEM	POSSIBLE CAUSE	SOLUTION
Sudden decrease in water flow rate	Obstructions in the supply line, preventing water from being pulled into the pump	Shut the pump off immediately, to prevent it from overheating and burning out. Check for blockages in both the pump and the skimmer strainer baskets.
Pump runs but doesn't pump	Low water level in the pool; a clogged filter; damage to the impeller inside the pump; air leaks in intake lines	If the pump is hot, shut it off immediately to avoid burnout. Check the water level and add more water if needed. Check the filter, and clean or replace it. If the pump still does not work, call a technician to check for impeller damage or air leaks.
Leaking pump	A deteriorated seal around the pump shaft	Replace the seal according to the instructions in the owner's manual.
Noisy pump	An oversized new pump, which is trying to discharge more water than is coming in; something jammed inside the impeller of an old pump	If the pump is oversized for the piping system (see pages 84 to 85), switch to a smaller pump. If the pump is an older one, check the impeller and remove any obstructions according to the owner's manual.

Routine maintenance is the best defense against problems with water quality.

water quality

PROBLEM	POSSIBLE CAUSE	SOLUTION
Cloudy or milky water	Polluting residue from suntan lotion or other oils	Clean the skimmer baskets and filter, and operate the pump for a longer time. Superchlorinate the pool (see page 179), then add a clarifier, which causes suspended particles to settle.
	High pH, high alkalinity, or both	Test and adjust pH and total alkalinity.
Cloudy, greenish water	Low chlorine levels, which allow algae to colonize the pool or spa	Superchlorinate the water with chlorine —to 10 ppm if the water is only slightly green and to 25 ppm if the water is solid green. Also brush the interior walls to remove algae, and clean the filter to remove dead algae.
Rust-colored water	Steel or iron fittings that have corroded because of low pH	Replace any metal fittings with copper or plastic piping. Then drain or dilute the rust-colored water— contact your pool installer to find out how to do this safely. Remove any rust stains from pool surfaces with a tile-and-liner cleaner. Make sure the fresh water you add is properly balanced.
Eye or throat irritation	A too-acidic or too-alkaline pH	Test and correct pH. To lower it, add dry acid daily according to packaging instructions until the proper pH reading is obtained. To raise the pH, add soda ash in the same way.
	Too many chloramines in the water	Superchlorinate.
Bathers' blond or tinted hair turns green	High levels of copper in the pool, either from an algicide or from copper pipes corroding because of low pH	Check the pH and raise it if necessary. If too much algicide has been added, add more water to bring the pool or spa into balance.

structural repairs

Although good swimming pools and spas are built to last, occasional mishaps can cause damage to the shell, requiring patching. In most cases, it's best to seek the assistance of a professional so that no additional damage is caused.

SEARCHING FOR LEAKS

Before you can repair a leak, you've got to find it. It's often difficult to determine whether a drop in the pool's water level is the result of a leak or normal evaporation. You can call in a professional leak detector to make the diagnosis, but first perform a "bucket test" yourself.

Fill a bucket three-quarters full with water and mark the water line on the inside of the bucket; also mark the water line on the wall of the pool. Let the bucket float in the pool—with the handle removed for better stability—for two or three days, keeping swimmers away. If the water loss is due to evaporation, the water level in both the bucket and the pool will have gone down by the same amount; if it's due to a leak, the level of the pool will have dropped farther than the water in the bucket.

REPAIRING CRACKED CONCRETE

Just as with a basement wall or foundation, the concrete walls of a pool or spa can sometimes crack as the surrounding soil moves. Small cracks can be easily

A bucket test can determine whether a pool is leaking. If water in the pool disappears faster than it evaporates from the bucket, this may be a sign of trouble.

A small crack in the wall of a concrete pool, such as the one shown above, can sometimes be corrected. If the crack is longer than 2 feet, however, this can indicate structural problems that cannot be resolved simply by patching.

repaired, but larger ones may indicate structural problems that have to be corrected through excavation.

In general, a crack less than ¼ inch wide and shorter than 2 feet long can be repaired, although the process is time consuming. The pool must first be drained to below the level of the crack, something that should not be done without a professional's guidance—a drained shell can crack further or pop out of the ground. After draining, use a chisel to widen the crack slightly and remove loose material from the edges. Dampen the concrete and make a patching compound with Portland cement. Then work the compound into the crack with a mason's trowel and brush the patch with muriatic acid to create a smooth texture—a process called etching (see safety tip on page 190). Coat the entire surface with an epoxy-based paint so the patched area or areas won't be visible.

REPLASTERING

Daily contact with chemicals and exposure to outdoor elements can slowly dissolve the plaster coating in a concrete pool and cause it to chip in a process known as spalling. Although this does not pose a structural hazard, it is unsightly and can create jagged edges that harbor algae. You can repair spalling by patching, but it will recur. Eventually, you'll need to replaster, usually within 7 to 10 years of the pool's construction. A plasterer will first sandblast off the old plaster, to ensure that the new coat will adhere well.

RECOATING FIBERGLASS

Although fiberglass pools are extremely durable, their gelcoat surface may fade, turn dull, or stain. If the deterioration is limited to one small area, more gelcoat can be applied to that spot. But if the damage covers a large area, the pool may have to be drained and the entire shell recoated (draining should be done only under a professional's supervision). You can coat your fiberglass pool with epoxy paint instead of gelcoat to enhance its appearance.

To properly patch a small crack, drain the pool to below the level of the crack. In order to create a fresh edge for the patching material to adhere to, widen the crack with a chisel or other tool.

Once the crack has been widened slightly, dampen the concrete and work a patching compound containing Portland cement into the crack. After that, smooth the edges using a mason's trowel.

PATCHING A VINYL LINER

The lining of a vinyl pool can be torn easily, but small tears—less than 3 inches long—can also be repaired easily. In many cases, you can do it yourself rather than bring in a professional. Anything much longer than 3 inches may require replacing the entire liner.

The most common way to repair a torn vinyl liner is to drain the pool to just below the tear mark—being careful not to completely empty the pool, unless under a professional's supervision. Then patch the liner, similar to the way you patch a bicycle inner tube (see process at right). To make the repair, it is important to have a piece of material that is identical to the original pool material. To prepare for eventual patching needs, ask the installer to give you an extra piece of liner when the pool is constructed.

Some manufacturers make underwater patching kits. To use one of these kits, position the patch, then apply pressure from the center outward to squeeze out any water.

---

important!

In a vinyl-lined or fiberglass pool or spa, a bulge in the side may indicate either drainage or structural problems —both of which are major and will require excavation and possibly even replacement of the pool. If the bulge is sizable—more than 2 feet in diameter —immediately call the installer and don't swim in the pool until it's checked.

While large tears in a vinyl pool require that an entire new liner be installed, small tears such as the one above, measuring 3 inches or less, can successfully be repaired.

To begin the process, rough up the area with a piece of sandpaper. Then coat it with a solvent cement; also apply the cement to the back of the patch.

Once the solvent cement has dried and become tacky, cut the patch so it extends at least 3 inches on all sides of the tear. Apply the patch.

seasonal maintenance

In warmer climates, seasonal pool maintenance is virtually nonexistent. Except perhaps for boosting the temperature during cooler months, you can use your pool or spa year-round with no difficulty. In colder climates where water freezes, though, or even in temperate climates where a pool or spa will remain dormant for long periods, you need to take proper care of your investment and make sure it's ready for use when warm weather returns.

WINTERIZING

If you live in an area that experiences freezing temperatures, you'll need to clear the water out of your pool's plumbing at the end of the swimming season. Frozen water won't harm the pool structure itself, but it can damage the pipes. Use an air compressor to blow water out of the lines, following the manufacturer's instructions. Also drain as much water as possible from the heater and filter. If any water remains, add non-toxic antifreeze—which differs from automotive antifreeze and is available from pool-supply stores. Disconnect the pump and heater. Then disconnect, clean, and store any chemical feeders.

Thoroughly vacuum and clean the pool and empty the skimmer baskets. Close the valve on the skimmer line and lower the water level to about 18 inches below the coping. Superchlorinate to remove chloramines. Finally—and most important of all—tightly cover the pool or spa. This will keep debris from accumulating in the water, making it vastly easier to open the pool in the spring.

If you'll continue using your spa during the cold weather, just continue your regular maintenance. On days that are too cold for outdoor soaking, lower the thermostat but keep the circulation system running to prevent the pipes from freezing. In the event of a severe freeze, drain all the plumbing but leave the spa full.

OPENING FOR THE SEASON

If properly prepared for the winter, a pool or spa can be opened during the spring with minimum effort. The most essential step is to clean the surrounding area—hosing and sweeping dirt and debris away—before opening the cover. If you don't clean first, the winter's accumulation will empty into the pool.

Return the pool's water level to normal using a garden hose. Any equipment such as the pump or heater that was disconnected will need reconnecting. Open the valve on the skimmer line so that water flows through the circulation system again. When everything is functioning, balance the water by testing the pH and total alkalinity, and then superchlorinate. Run the pump 24 hours a day, reducing the run by an hour or two each day until the water is perfectly balanced; this may take a week or more.

from swimming pool to ice-skating rink

∎ ∎ ∎

If you live in an area that has at least two months of temperatures below freezing, you may be able to have your in-ground swimming pool do double duty as an ice-skating rink. To transform it, winterize the pool (see above left), lowering the water level as described. Float a large vinyl liner on the water that extends onto the deck for about 2 to 3 feet and hold it in place with water-filled plastic jugs or sandbags. Fill the liner with water to a depth of at least 4 inches and allow it to freeze solid. Four or more inches of ice won't harm the pool at all.

safe swimming

Along with the pleasure of owning a pool or spa comes a big responsibility: providing a safe environment for swimmers and nonswimmers alike. In part, this means keeping the water clean and free of debris, but it also means securing the area around the pool, encouraging responsible behavior, and providing constant supervision of children. Some safety measures may be mandated by your town's laws or by the terms of your insurance policy. Other crucial steps to ensure that your pool or spa remains a safe source of fun are up to you.

water smarts

According to the U.S. Consumer Product Safety Commission (CPSC), the vast majority of people who drown or suffer underwater injuries in a swimming pool are children under the age of five—and most often those accidents take place in pools owned by their parents, grandparents, or other close relatives. A young child can drown in less time than it takes to answer a telephone—or to read this sentence.

CHILD'S PLAY

Well-designed barriers can do quite a lot to keep children out of your pool area when no one is out there supervising (see page 206), but even the most secure fence doesn't guarantee safety. The fact is most child drownings and submersion injuries occur in the presence of one or both parents.

Fortunately, there are some steps you can take to ensure that your children and their pals can frolic to their hearts' content—and your peace of mind.

EARLY DOES IT If a pool figures in your future, make sure your youngsters learn to swim. The American Academy of Pediatrics recommends starting swim classes once your child reaches the age of four. Many organizations, including the Red Cross, the YMCA, and the YWCA, offer reasonably priced swimming classes for young children.

If your toddlers take swimming lessons in the spring, chances are they'll be swimming like fish by summer's end. But they may forget their new skills if they don't have the opportunity to swim over the winter. So if you close your pool for the cold months, be sure to either take your youngsters to an indoor pool every couple of weeks for practice sessions or sign them up for some refresher lessons the following spring.

Water games can provide hours of fun for swimmers of all ages, but make sure you set rules for safe play—and see that everyone obeys them.

DON'T COUNT ON TOYS Rafts, inner tubes, and inflatable animals can give your youngsters hours of fun in the water. And wearable flotation devices such as water wings and float suits can boost the confidence of budding swimmers. But never rely on these playthings as substitutes for serious safety equipment—and your own eagle-eyed attentiveness.

KEEP WATCH As most parents are well aware, small children are agile, fearless, and fast. But even older kids who are good swimmers should be carefully watched when they're in or near the pool. If you have to leave the area—even for a second or two—take the kids with you. When you have a pool party, arrange for "designated watchers" to supervise the children. Better yet, hire a professional lifeguard to be on duty.

BE PREPARED When a pool accident happens, a fast response is crucial. Be sure to learn water rescue techniques, artificial respiration, and cardiopulmonary

resuscitation (CPR), and keep your skills up to date by taking refresher courses. Make sure that all babysitters, including grandparents and older siblings, do the same. (YMCA and YWCA lifeguard courses include all these rescue procedures.) In addition to other safety equipment (see page 205), keep a cordless or cellular telephone beside the pool, programmed with emergency numbers.

RULES FOR POOLS

When you own a pool or spa, setting a few simple rules can spell the difference between hours of nagging worry and countless days of pleasure and relaxation. Here are some guidelines to enforce:
- No running around the pool.
- No unsupervised children in or around the pool.
- No glass containers at poolside.
- No drinking alcohol while using the pool.

important!

A lightning strike can be deadly. Clear the pool at the first sound of thunder or if you know that a storm is close by, and do not let anyone go back into the water for at least 20 minutes after the last thunderclap.

diving dos and don'ts
■ ■ ■

WHEN DIVING INTO THE WATER, DO:
- *Plan your dive path. Know the shape and depth of the pool as well as the location of other swimmers and objects that are on or under the surface.*
- *Learn and practice proper diving techniques. Hold your head and arms up and steer with your hands. If you're using a board, dive straight ahead from the end, not off the side.*
- *Before you dive, bounce lightly on the board to check its spring.*
- *Aim for the surface. Shallow dives are the only safe kind to do in home pools. Deep vertical dives, like the ones competitive divers perform, require specially designed pools with very deep water throughout.*
- *Yield the right of way to swimmers already in the water.*

TO AVOID INJURY, DON'T:
- *Dive alone.*
- *Drink alcohol and dive.*
- *Dive into an above-ground pool.*
- *Dive into shallow water or across narrow parts of a pool.*
- *Play or roughhouse on the diving board.*
- *Try backflips or fancy dives.*
- *Dive through inner tubes or other floating objects.*

around the pool

Living next to any body of water poses certain risks. That's true even if your aquatic territory consists of a spa little bigger than a bathtub. In addition to installing nonslip decking (see page 144) and adequate lighting (pages 170 to 173), following a few basic precautions will enhance safety.

Clear, clean water makes for delightful—and worry-free—dips in the pool.

A pool deck that's open and free of clutter ensures safe passage for swimmers and nonswimmers alike.

HAZARDS TO ELIMINATE

When you put people and pools together, trouble can brew in a hurry. Here are some of the most common causes of problems, along with commonsense ways of avoiding them.

TOO MANY SWIMMERS Amid the noise and confusion of an overcrowded pool, a swimmer in distress can easily go unnoticed. In addition, the presence of a large, excited "audience" can encourage many children as well as some adults to show off and take dangerous chances. Limit the number of people that can be in the pool at any one time, and encourage rest periods. During pool parties, a timeout of 10 to 15 minutes every hour will calm excited children and settle the nerves of supervising grownups.

CLUTTER Sports equipment and safety gear on the pool deck are tripping hazards, and toys present a double danger: not only are they potential stumbling blocks but, in or out of the pool, they're magnets for young children, who can easily fall into the water. Even furniture can pose risks: if a chair or a table is close to the edge, children may be tempted to use it as a diving board. Keep rescue equipment stowed in its proper place until it's needed. Put away toys, sports equipment, and other objects when they're not in use. Keep all furniture, planters, and accessories well away from the edge of the pool. Be sure the pool or spa cover is completely removed to prevent entrapment.

ELECTRICITY It's important to remember that electricity and water don't mix. Use only GFCI-protected outlets around the pool or spa, and don't install any outlet within 10 feet of the water. Choose battery-operated appliances or electrical models that are approved for use outdoors and near water. And keep all appliances, including radios and CD players, far enough away that they can't fall or be pulled into the water. Don't touch any electrical appliance while you're wet, especially if you're in contact with something metal, such as a pool ladder. (It's okay to use a cellular or wireless phone while you're in a pool or spa, but never use a regular telephone.) If an appliance does fall into the water, unplug it before you try to retrieve it. And always hire a qualified, licensed electrician to perform electrical repairs on pool or spa equipment.

POORLY MAINTAINED WATER Safe swimming demands clear, sanitary water. The water in your pool or spa should have the correct chemical balance, be free of any leaves and other debris, and be clear enough that you can see the bottom.

EQUIPPED FOR SAFETY

When trouble strikes, having basic rescue equipment at hand can make a world of difference in your ability to respond. Pool-equipment suppliers and marinas sell a variety of devices that make it easier to reach swimmers in distress and pull them to safety. Whatever gear you choose, keep it easily accessible and ready to use. Inspect all pieces regularly and replace them at the first sign of wear and tear. Here are some must-haves for any pool:

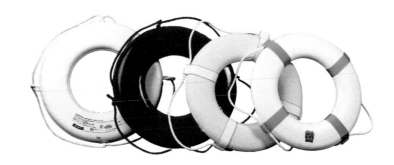

RING BUOY This classic piece of rescue equipment is designed to be thrown to a conscious victim who can hold on while being pulled to safety. Choose a buoy with a rope that's at least as long as half the width of your pool at its widest point. Better yet, get two buoys and keep one on each side of the pool, with the line coiled and ready for use. And don't be tempted to use an inner tube or other inflatable toy for a water rescue.

SHEPHERD'S CROOK At 12 to 16 feet long, this pole extends your reach considerably; the half-circle at the end lets you draw in an unconscious victim floating on or below the surface.

RESCUE TUBE This flexible vinyl-coated foam tube, often with a hook at one end, can be wrapped around a victim. The attached nylon tow rope has a shoulder strap to make towing easier.

safety tip

When you're shopping for safety gear, be sure to pick up or put together a first-aid kit. Keep it within easy reach, and make sure everyone who uses your pool knows where to find it.

safe sliding

A water slide can give children—and young-at-heart grownups—hours of fun. But as with diving boards, it's crucial to follow basic safety procedures. The process starts with a call to your contractor or a pool technician, who can help you choose the best model for your pool. Location is important. Place the slide where water is deep enough so that people who use the slide won't hit their feet on the pool bottom, because leg fractures can result. But if you place the structure in very deep water, you'll want to restrict its use to good swimmers. Once you've installed your slide (or better yet, had it professionally installed), issue these guidelines for all would-be sliders:

- If the slide does not empty into deep water, have all users slide in a seated position, feet first. If the water is deep, sliders may safely go down lying flat, belly down, head first, and hands out in front.
- No one may use the slide as a diving board, no matter how securely it is fastened to the deck.
- Only one person at a time may use the slide.
- As with diving, swimmers already in the water have the right of way.
- No clowning around or roughhousing on the slide.

restricting access

An unfenced, uncovered pool or spa is a tragedy waiting to happen. Most towns and cities have laws requiring some sort of protective barrier, although the specific details vary. Even if you live deep in the country, with no fencing mandates and no human neighbors for miles around, a good, solid fence or wall and a sturdy cover for your pool or spa are the best safety investments you can make.

VERTICAL BARRIERS

The guidelines below, established by the U.S. Consumer Product Safety Commission, are the minimum requirements for keeping young children from going over, under, or through a pool barrier. Because legal requirements can differ from community to community, check with your local building department before installing a fence or wall.

FENCES AND WALLS

- The barrier, whether a fence or wall, should completely surround the pool. If your house forms part of the barrier, the doors leading to the pool should have alarms in place or the pool should have a power safety cover (see "Alarms and Covers," page 208).
- The fence or wall should be at least 48 inches high, with no openings or projections (including crossbars) that a young child could use as a foot- or handhold.
- The bottom of the barrier should be no more than 4 inches above the ground on the side facing away from the pool.
- Vertical fence slats should be less than 4 inches apart.
- In a chain-link or lattice fence, no opening should be more than 1¾ inches wide.

GATES

- Gates should be self-closing and self-latching; they should close in the direction of the pool (so a child who pushes against an open gate will close it).
- If the latch-release mechanism is less than 54 inches from the bottom of the gate, it should be at least 3 inches below the top of the gate on the side facing the pool (thereby preventing a child from reaching over the top to spring the latch).
- Within 18 inches of the latch-release mechanism, no opening on the fence or gate should exceed ½ inch. This will prevent children from reaching small fingers through an opening to release the latch.

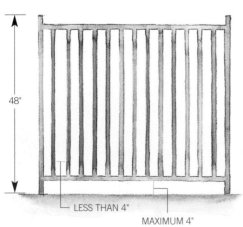

48"

LESS THAN 4"

MAXIMUM 4"

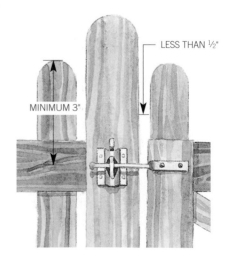

LESS THAN ½"

MINIMUM 3"

Whether metal, wood, or some other material, a fence offers security and peace of mind. Eliminate temptations to climb by keeping garbage cans, furniture, and other gear away from the outside of the fence.

This Katchakid cover is made of strong vinyl mesh. With openings only 4" wide, it's designed to serve as a barrier for children who tumble—or leap—into the pool. The openings allow water to drain through.

ALARMS AND COVERS

When your house serves as part of the pool barrier, door alarms or a pool power safety cover are essential equipment. For extra insurance, it makes good sense to have both (and in some places the law requires it).

ALARMS As with fences, the legal requirements regarding alarms differ from one community to the next. However, these are the minimum standards recommended by the CPSC:

- Every door leading to the pool area should be equipped with an alarm that sounds for at least 30 seconds whenever the door is opened.
- The alarm should be loud (at least 85 decibels when measured 10 feet away from the door) and distinct from other household sounds, such as telephones, doorbells, and smoke alarms.
- The alarm should have an automatic reset feature.
- To allow adults to pass through the door, the alarm should have a switch that deactivates the mechanism for up to 15 seconds; the switch should be installed at least 54 inches above the door's threshold.

SAFETY COVERS Don't confuse pool safety covers with covers that are designed simply to keep the water warm and free of debris. Such covers do nothing to ensure safety. In fact, they can be more hazardous than leaving a pool uncovered, since a child (or pet) who falls or jumps onto a lightweight cover will cause it to collapse, and may easily be trapped in the water-filled folds and drown. Whether you choose a motor-driven safety cover or one that you roll on and off using a hand crank, look for a cover that:

- Meets Standard F1346-91 of the American Society for Testing and Materials (ASTM). Such a cover will support the weight of two adults and a child (roughly 400 pounds), thus permitting an easy rescue should someone fall onto it.
- Is made of tough mesh netting that lets water drain through. This is a crucial consideration, since a young child can drown in less than an inch of water.
- Has no gaps along the perimeter through which a small child could crawl.

SPA COVERS Spa covers are primarily designed to keep heat in and litter out. But if you have children or pets on the scene, make sure the barrier will support their weight—and yours—in the event of an accident. A spa cover should meet the same weight-bearing standards as a pool cover.

A rigid spa cover that's intended to prevent accidental drownings should support about 400 pounds, just like a pool safety cover.

With their raised sides, above-ground pools can foil even the most determined toddler. Still, it's best to go the extra mile and add a sturdy (and good-looking) fence.

SECURING ABOVE-GROUND POOLS

A typical above-ground pool, whose sides reach up 48 inches or so, serves as its own barrier. Still, extra protection is always a good idea—and may be mandated by local law. Deck kits made for above-ground pools usually include a 36-inch-high fence. Or you can purchase fencing from the pool's manufacturer and mount it on top of the pool wall. From the standpoint of a small child, that leaves only one possible point of entry to the pool: the stairs. To eliminate that weak link in your security system, either enclose the stairs with a fence and gate that meet the standards listed on page 206, or remove the stairs when the pool is not in use.

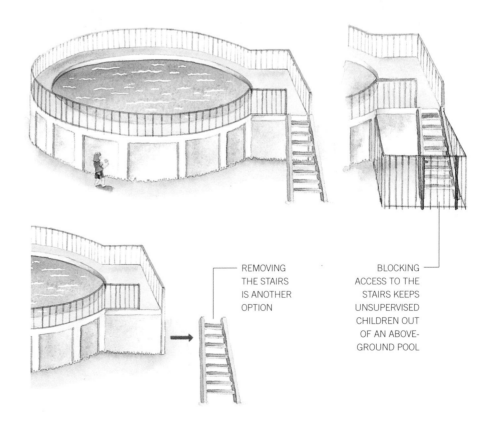

REMOVING THE STAIRS IS ANOTHER OPTION

BLOCKING ACCESS TO THE STAIRS KEEPS UNSUPERVISED CHILDREN OUT OF AN ABOVE-GROUND POOL

the allure of the sauna

Whereas swimming pools and spas let you experience the pleasure of bathing in water, saunas provide the physical and mental exhilaration of being bathed in heat. Not only are they sources of much-needed physical renewal, they're also wonderful places for quiet contemplation.

FROM OUT OF THE PAST

Ancient Finland was the birthplace of the sauna, and modern-day Finland continues to enjoy it as a vital part of the culture. The traditional heat source is wood, which is burned to heat a pile of volcanic rocks inside a wooden room. When the fire dies down the sauna is ready to be used. To correct the low humidity, water is ladled over the rocks, which causes an explosion of steam to rise into the room. Because of the high heat, people don't usually linger long—after 5 to 10 minutes, everyone heads outdoors to take a dip in a cool pond or stream or to roll in the snow. Then they go back into the sauna, where they gently massage their skin with small bundles of birch twigs known as *vihtas* to stimulate circulation. After using the sauna, most bathers rest in order to cool down, and then have a light snack called a *saunapala*.

BENEFITS TO YOUR HEALTH

Besides providing a pleasurable way to relax, saunas also stimulate circulation through the cycle of perspiration, rapid cooling, and rest. Perspiring heavily may help to clean clogged pores, resulting in skin with a healthier glow. Some people believe that saunas also help temporarily reduce muscular and nervous tension, and may even heighten mental awareness. In addition, doctors sometimes prescribe spending time in a sauna for patients with arthritis or rheumatism, because the heat of the sauna can temporarily reduce inflammation in muscles and joints. Saunas can also provide temporary relief for the common cold by clearing uncomfortable sinus congestion. As with anything, however, moderation is essential when using a sauna. Read the cautions on page 217, and be sure to talk to your doctor if you have specific concerns or questions.

With an eye toward design, a sauna can be as appealing on the outside as it is inviting on the inside.

anatomy of a sauna

Although saunas vary greatly, all contain two essential elements—the insulated sauna room itself and the stove used to heat it.

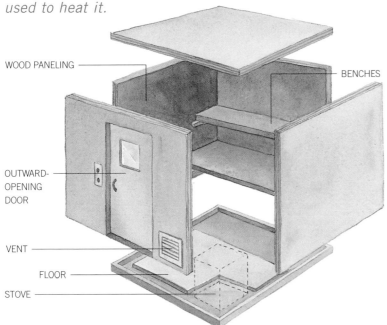

WOOD PANELING

BENCHES

OUTWARD-OPENING DOOR

VENT

FLOOR

STOVE

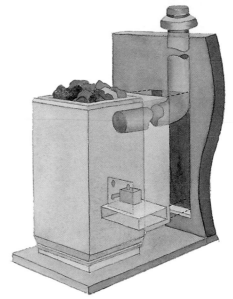

GAS STOVES These stoves come in many styles, including those with electronic ignition, which is preferable to a pilot light. They heat up quickly, are relatively inexpensive to operate, and are a good option for homes already connected to a gas line.

SAUNA ROOMS

The sauna room is an insulated wooden box, usually rectangular, that features two or three tiers of wooden benches for reclining. In most cases, the stove (see below) holds a load of special volcanic rock—often imported from Finnish quarries—that releases a gentle and even heat. The ideal ceiling height for a sauna is about 7 feet—tall enough for most people to stand comfortably yet low enough to limit the volume of space to be heated. The interior is paneled with unfinished wood, which will stay pleasingly warm to the touch, unlike metal or plastic.

SAUNA STOVES

Modern sauna stoves can be fueled by wood, gas, or electricity. Each has its advantages.

WOOD STOVES These traditional stoves are an excellent option, particularly for outdoor saunas, but they do require a steady supply of wood. Be aware that they're banned in many locations by local building codes.

ELECTRIC STOVES
These are the most convenient, as well as the most popular, stoves. In most models, heating coils are located beneath the rocks. Be sure to get a model that allows you to splash water on the rocks—as wood and gas stoves do. The resulting steam is an essential element in a true Finnish-style heat bath.

213

installing a sauna

When choosing your sauna, size and shape are the two most important elements to consider. Saunas can be built from scratch or from a precut kit or prefabricated model.

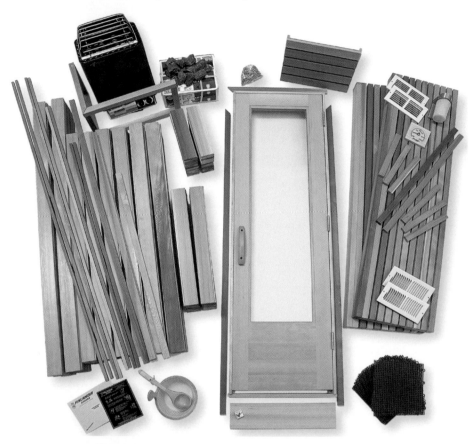

LOCATING THE SAUNA

As with a swimming pool or spa, placing your sauna in the right location is essential to its success. If you choose to have it in your home, it's desirable to locate it near a dressing room as well as a bathroom with a shower. One popular location for saunas is a walk-in closet next to the master bathroom. Other options are out-of-the-way areas of the house, such as a corner of the basement, the attic, a spare bedroom, or even part of the garage.

If you prefer to have your sauna outdoors, you can install it in a cabana or pool house to take advantage of existing changing rooms or showers. If you don't have a pool, you can tuck the sauna into an unused area of the yard, which can be landscaped with trees and shrubs for additional privacy. When planning an outdoor sauna, remember to factor in the cost of site prepara-

The first step in piecing together a sauna kit is to construct the outer frame, as shown above.

Precut tongue-and-groove boards slide into position in the frame to form the sauna's walls and ceiling.

The door arrives prehung, which allows you to easily install its frame into one of the walls.

tion, wiring, and any gas or electrical connections.

Whether indoors or out, allow 2 feet of bench space for each seated person (6 feet per person for reclining). For a single person, the smallest sauna would measure about 3 by 4 feet; a sauna for four people might measure 5 by 7 feet. A sauna approximately 8 by 10 feet could hold eight or nine people if benches were built on multiple levels.

BUILDING A CUSTOM SAUNA

If you're looking for a custom design, an experienced architect or a designer can create a unique sauna with a distinctive finish that will suit your particular space. Custom-designed saunas offer the greatest flexibility in terms of shape, bench layout, and materials, and can be made to look like part of your house, rather than a separate unit. As with all custom work, though, hiring a professional

to design your sauna is the most expensive approach; costs can range from a few thousand dollars to more than $10,000 for elaborate units.

MANUFACTURED SAUNAS

Far less expensive and easier to install than custom designs, manufactured saunas come in precut and prefabricated versions. Most manufacturers will make some custom modifications, such as a specific interior or exterior finish or a change in the dimensions or configuration of benches. Most precut kits include all the materials needed to construct a sauna, including the exterior roofing and siding for outdoor installations and precut tongue-and-groove lumber for the walls and ceilings. However, some manufacturers provide the materials for the interior only. In this case, you must build the framing according to instructions, as well as add

insulation and provide a waterproof floor. Most manufacturers will supply the stove, although you may have to order it separately.

In addition to precut kits, prefabricated systems are also available. These are complete modular units, with finished interiors and exteriors, that are shipped in pieces and assembled easily. Wiring for lights is already in place, and electric stoves or heaters are usually included, though they'll need to be installed and connected by an electrician. Prefabricated saunas usually come in easy-to-handle packages, with their parts numbered to coordinate with step-by-step assembly instructions. Assembly usually requires only simple tools, such as a hammer and screwdriver, plus a co-worker to help muscle everything into place.

Sauna costs vary greatly, but using a kit or a prefabricated system will usually save you money. A simple unit for one or two people might cost between $1,500 and $2,000. Larger units will cost considerably more. For instance, a sauna big enough to hold eight or nine people might cost well over $7,500.

Once the sauna shell is pieced together correctly, each of the boards is nailed securely into place.

The roof can be added next. This is sometimes an extra item that is not included in a precut kit.

smart tip

For many people, the process of taking a sauna is an acquired taste. Before you buy a sauna, try one out not just once but several times to make sure you'll enjoy it.

enjoying your sauna

Unlike a dip in the pool or a soak in the spa, a session in the sauna should be carefully choreographed to make the most of the sauna's benefits. Instead of squeezing your sojourn into a few spare minutes, try to spend a longer period in the heat and follow it with a cool-down and rest. If you repeat the process several times, the relaxing effect will be magnified.

"CURING" A NEW SAUNA

You'll need to properly cure a new sauna before taking your first heat bath. To begin the process, remove any construction debris or sawdust by sweeping the interior, then vacuum and wipe the inside surfaces with a damp cloth. Also wash the heating rocks in the stove to keep any sand from ending up on the floor. The first time you turn on the stove, let it run for 30 minutes with the door open. This will help vent any noxious odors that result when protective coatings on the stove burn off. After a half hour, close the door and set the temperature as high as possible—usually about 200 degrees—and leave it that way for five or six hours. At that point the sauna is ready to use, and you can adjust the temperature to where you like it.

USING YOUR SAUNA

Following the traditional sequence of bathing in heat and then cooling down can accentuate the sauna experience. To begin, prewarm the sauna. Most electric saunas take about 30 minutes to reach their full heat, which is between 150 and 195 degrees. Before you step in, take a quick shower, then enter and sit or recline on a bench. At first, the humidity in the sauna will be low—about 5 to 10 percent—but it will gradually increase

as you perspire. You can also increase the humidity by ladling water over the hot rocks, which produces a burst of steam. The steam will greatly heighten the effect of the heat and also increase perspiration.

When you leave the sauna, cool down by taking a shower or a quick swim. Some people enjoy having a brief rest before returning to the sauna. If that's your preference, lie down for approximately the same amount of time as you spent in the sauna. After cooling down or resting, head back to the sauna, and repeat the entire process two or three times. End the final heat bath with a gentle loofah scrub—the modern equivalent of massaging with *vihtas*—then have a rest followed by a light snack.

SAUNA MAINTENANCE

Saunas, unlike swimming pools and spas, require very little maintenance. After using your sauna, turn off the stove and open the door to allow the wood surfaces to dry thoroughly. Wash the inside of the sauna every few months with a damp cloth and a cleanser or disinfectant recommended by the manufacturer. Electric and gas stoves need little if any maintenance; wood stoves will require occasional soot removal as recommended by the manufacturer.

Attention to location and layout will increase a sauna's desirability. This outdoor sauna, left, benefits from being located in between a shower and a spa—both of which can be used for cool-downs and rests.

With minimal maintenance, such as leaving the door open to cool down and dry out the inside after use, a sauna can remain fresh-looking even after years of steady use.

safety first

■ ■ ■

Appealing as they are, saunas aren't for everyone, since certain medical and physical conditions can be aggravated by exposure to heat. Check with a physician before you take a sauna if you:

■ have high blood pressure, respiratory disease, serious circulatory problems, or a chronic illness such as diabetes

■ are pregnant

■ are taking antibiotics, tranquilizers, stimulants, or any other drug that might be affected by an increase in metabolism

In addition, keep in mind that alcohol and saunas don't mix. And remember that if for any reason you begin to feel dizzy, nauseated, or uncomfortably hot while you're in the sauna, or if your pulse starts to beat abnormally fast, you should exit immediately.

resources

ASSOCIATIONS

National Spa & Pool Institute
2111 Eisenhower Ave.
Alexandria, VA 22314
703-838-0083
www.nspi.org

National Swimming Pool Foundation
224 East Cheyenne Mountain Blvd.
Colorado Springs, CO 80906
719-540-9119
www.nspf.com

POOLS

Delair Group
8600 River Rd.
Delair, NJ 08110
800-235-0185, 856-663-2900
www.delairgroup.com
Above-ground pools, fences

Paco Pools & Spas
784 Merrick Rd.
Baldwin, NY 11510
516-546-1400
www.pacopoolsandspas.com
Vinyl-lined and gunite pools, pool chemicals

Raynor Pools
1460 Montank Hwy.
East Patchogue, NY 11772-5300
866-472-9667
www.raynorpools.com
Vinyl-lined pools; heater, pump, and filter parts; covers

San Juan Pools
West Coast:
850 North Davidson St.
Eloy, AZ 85231
866-535-7946

East Coast:
2302 Lasso Lane
Lakeland, FL 33801
800-535-7946

www.sanjuanpools.com
Fiberglass pools and equipment

SCP Pool Corp.
877-407-POOL
www.backyardescape.com
A wholesaler whose web site offers a directory of in-ground pool installers, above-ground pool dealers, and equipment dealers.

Viking Pools
California, Texas, Florida, West Virginia
800-854-7665
www.vikingpools.net
Fiberglass pools

PORTABLE SPAS, HOT TUBS, SAUNAS

Aqua Swim 'N' Spa
P.O. Box 3707
Brownsville, TX 78523
956-831-2715
www.rioplastics.com
Swim spas, physiotherapy spas

Callaway Woodworks
11320-A FM 529
Houston, TX 77041
877-518-9698
www.callawaywoodworks.com
Hot tubs, saunas, accessories

Dimension One Spas
2611 Business Park Dr.
Vista, CA 92081
800-345-7727
www.d1spas.com
Portable spas

Finlandia Sauna Products, Inc.
14010-B S.W. 72nd Ave.
Portland, OR 97224-0088
800-354-3342
www.finlandiasauna.com
Finnish saunas and accessories

Northern Lights Cedar Hot Tubs
4122 Henderson Hwy.
Winnipeg, Manitoba
R2E 1B3 Canada
204-228-5867
www.cedartubs.com
Cedar hot tubs and saunas

Saunafin
115 Bowes Rd., #2
Concord, Ontario
L4K 1H7 Canada
800-387-7029
www.saunafin.com
*Sauna kits, prefab saunas,
accessories*

SwimEx, Inc.
373 Market St.
Warren, RI 02885-0328
800-877-7946
www.swimex.com
*Swim spas, aquatic therapy pools,
water exercise equipment*

MECHANICAL EQUIPMENT
Hayward Pool Products
900 Fairmount Ave.
Elizabeth, NJ 07207
908-351-5400
www.haywardnet.com
Filters, valves, heaters, pumps, cleaners

Pentair Pool Products
East Coast:
1620 Hawkins Ave.
Sanford, NC 27330
800-831-7133

West Coast:
10951 W. Los Angeles Ave.
Moorpark, CA 93021
800-831-7133
www.pentairpool.com
Pumps, heaters, filters

Raypak
2151 Eastman Ave.
Oxnard, CA 93030
805-278-5300
www.raypak.com
Pool and spa heaters

Solar Living
P.O. Box 12
Netcong, NJ 07857
973-691-8483
www.capturethesun.com
Solar-pool heating

CLEANING AND MAINTENANCE
AquaChek
P.O. Box 4659
Elkhart, IN 46514-0659
574-262-2060
www.aquachek.com
Test strips and kits

Floatron
P.O. Box 51000
Phoenix, AZ 85076
480-345-2222
www.floatron.com
Solar-powered ionizer

Polaris Pool Systems
2620 Commerce Way
Vista, CA 92081-8438
800-822-7933
www.polarispool.com
Automatic cleaners, chlorinators,
accessories

Recreation Supply Co.
P.O. Box 2757
Bismarck, ND 58502-2757
800-437-8072
www.recsupply.com
Water testing, pool cleaners,
leaf skimmers

Specialty Pool Products
110 Main St.
Broad Brook, CT 06016-0388
800-983-7665
www.poolproducts.com
Cleaners, spa covers, heaters,
filters, lighting

ACCESSORIES
Cover Pools, Inc.
800-447-2838
www.coverpools.com
Safety, solar, and automatic
covers

Katchakid
1737 Stebbins Dr., #220
Houston, TX 77043
888-552-8242
Child safety-net cover

Recreation Supply Co.
(see Cleaning and Maintenance)
Water sports, safety and rescue
equipment, lighting, handrails,
ladders, slides

Recreonics
4200 Schmitt Ave.
Louisville, KY 40213
800-428-3254
www.recreonics.com
Pool lifts, ramps, aquatic wheelchairs

S.R. Smith
P.O. Box 400
Canby, OR 97013
800-824-4387
www.srsmith.com
Slides, diving boards, ladders, rails

Water Gear
P.O. Box 759
Pismo Beach, CA 93448-0759
800-794-6432
www.watergear.com
Water toys, flotation aids, water games

LIGHTING AND LANDSCAPING
Cabana Village, LLC
501 Silverside Rd., #105
Wilmington, DE 19809
800-959-3808
www.cabanavillage.com
Sheds, pool houses, spa enclosures

Fiberstars, Inc.
44259 Nobel Dr.
Fremont, CA 94538
800-327-7877
www.fiberstars.com
Fiber-optic lighting

Pentair Pool Products
(see Mechanical Equipment)
Incandescent lighting

Trex
800-289-8739
www.trex.com
Decking and railing made of recycled
plastic and wood

credits

PHOTOGRAPHY AND ILLUSTRATION

Palma Allen: 122, 123 all, 124 all, 125 both; Courtesy of Arch Wood Co.: 142T, 164B; **Liz Ball, Positive Images:** 192; Marion Brenner: 106, 116; **Gay Bumgarner, Positive Images:** 166T; Karen Bussolini: 150T; Karen Bussolini, Positive Images: 13T, 35B, 48, 50, 56B, 93TL, 138, 156, 184, 204L; Courtesy of Cabana Village, LLC; photo by John Gardner: 92; Courtesy of Callaway Woodworks: 75T; Glenn Christiansen: 175BR; Courtesy of Cover-Pools, Inc.: 95; Crandall & Crandall: 55, 132 both, 133; Courtesy of Delair Pools Group: 20B; Ken Druse: 148; Phillip H. Ennis: 8, 18T, 25B, 41T, 47T, 66, 81, 100B, 130, 144BR, 163T, 171, 174R; Derek Fell: 14B, 16, 98B, 134, 149L, 204R; Cheryl Fenton: 117, 128B, 129, 135R, 143, 146T, 169TL, 169ML, 169R, 172TL, 172TM, 172TR, 172BL, 172BM, 173 all, 179, 180 both, 182, 185, 188 all, 189, 190 all, 196 both, 197 both, 198 all, 205TL; Courtesy of Finlandia Sauna: 212, 214T, 216, 217; **Ron Gibbons Swimming Pools, Courtesy of Fiberstars, Inc.:** 170; John Granen: 23B; Steven Gunther: 2, 22, 24B, 26T, 31L, 36, 54B, 57 all, 68, 69R, 72, 109B, 136, 137, 141, 154, 155R, 157; Ken Gutmaker: 45MR, 113T; Jerry Harpur: 9T, 10, 11T, 17 both, 54T, 70, 71, 85, 86, 93R, 127B, 186; Lynne Harrison: 210; Saxon Holt: 1, 9B, 11B, 20T, 40R, 43, 58, 135L, 153B, 160, 164M, 172BR, 175ML; J-C. Hurni: 14T, 15 both, 31R, 62, 64, 65, 67, 93BL, 110, 114, 115, 119T; Courtesy of Katchakid, Inc.: 208T; Rene Klein: 78, 108,

109T, 113B; Dennis Krukowski: 28; Allan Mandell: 13BL, 18B, 74T, 140B, 142B, 147 both, 152, 155L, 208B; Charles Mann: 153T; Rik Olson: 159; Courtesy of Paco Pools & Spas, Ltd.: 60; Jerry Pavia: 13BR, 105L, 127T, 207BL; Courtesy of Pentair Pool Products: 82, 84T, 88, 89 both, 96L, 101B; Courtesy of Polaris Pool Systems: 96M, 96R; Courtesy of Raynor Pools, Inc.: 119B; Courtesy of RayPak: 105R; Courtesy of Recreational Supply Co.: 205TR, 205BL; Susan A. Roth: 6, 21T, 76, 94, 126, 175TR, 203R; Courtesy of San Juan Pools: 121B, 218; Courtesy of Saunafin: 214BL, 214BM, 214BR, 215 both; Courtesy of SCP Pool Corp.; photo by M. Thomas Blake: 209; Courtesy of S.R. Smith: 98T, 99, 100T, 101T, 181, 205BR; Courtesy of Solar Living, Inc.: 90; Thomas J. Story: 21B, 128T, 146BL, 146BM, 146MR, 146BR; Tim Street-Porter: 12, 19, 23T, 26B, 35T, 37, 38, 42, 52, 83, 140T, 144ML, 162, 164T, 174L, 195, 200; Courtesy of SwimEx: 75B; Courtesy of Trex Co., Inc.: 145B; Mark Turner: 33L, 161T; Brian Vanden Brink: 25T, 27, 45TR, 74B, 97, 104, 149R, 163B, 166B, 183, 191; Courtesy of Viking Pools: 111, 121T; Jessie Walker: 30, 41B, 73B; Deidra Walpole: 24T, 32, 33R, 40L, 47B, 56T, 59, 69L, 73T, 79, 84B, 102, 144BL, 145T, 168 both, 176, 178, 207T, 207BR; Courtesy of Water Gear, Inc.: 202; Lee Anne White, Positive Images: 161B; Peter Whiteley: 150B

DESIGN

Audio Command Systems: 66; Heide Stolpstead Baldwin: 153B; Liv Ballard: 23T; Charlie Barnet: 45MR; Moses Becker: 144ML; Barry Beer: 86; Tom Beeton: 83;

Axel Berg: 27, 191; Michael Buccino Assoc.: 154; Martyn Lawrence Bullard: 4BM, 164T, 200; Pamela Burton: 36; Charyl Butenko Garden Design: 13BL, 140B, 142B, 147B; Pedro Castillo: 175BR; Lim Chang: 47T; Chary & Siguenza: 163T; Steve Chase: 17T; Linda Chisari: 207BL; Thomas Church: 58; Todd Cole Designs: 4TR, 106; Wayne Connor: 4BL, 85, 186; Robert Cornell: 68; Nancy Corzine: 130; Country Floors: 144BR, 174R; Conni Cross: 211, 148, 175TR, 203R; Grover Dear: 127B; Topher Delaney: 11T, 175BR; Mayita Dinos Garden Design: 207BR; Garret Eckbo for Sam Hellinger USA: 54T; Mary Effron: 10, 137, 141; Filion & Castonguay: 119T; Kathy Fleming: 3TL, 6; Ray Forsum: 132 both, 133; Glenn Fries: 56B; Sonny Garcia: 172BR; Michael Glassman & Assoc.: 150B; Frank Glynn: 13BR; Frank Gravino: 138; Green Scene Land-scape Design: 168T; Greenbaum Interiors/Lynn Cone: 25B; John Herbst, Jr., and Assoc.: 55; Tom Hobbs: 155L; Ann Clark Holt Design: 4BR, 210; Horiuchi & Solien: 74B, 104, 149R, 163B; J-C. Hurni: 110, 114; J-C. Hurni and M. Havlin: 115; Mark Hutker & Assoc.: 97; Johnsen Landscapes & Pools: 156, 204L; Kappe + Du Architects: 21B; Kennedy Landscape Design Assoc.: 24T, 32, 73T, 79, 145T; John Kenyon: 23B; KJS Interiors: 171; Brian J. Koribanick, Landscape Techniques, Inc.: 3TR, 28; Gordon Kurtis Landscape Design: 3BR, 176; Michael LaRocca: 18T; Jerry Leeds: 8; Mia Lehrer & Assoc.: 22, 24B, 26T, 54B, 57T, 155R; Lucinda Lester: 109B, 136; Mark David Levine Landscape Design Group: 33R, 40L, 56T, 59, 168B; Mel Light: 17B; M. Martel: 15 both; John Marton: 25T; Clark Matschek: 18B, 105L, 147T; Jeff Mendoza: 9T; John Morris

index

Page numbers in **boldface** refer to photograph captions